STUFF HIPSTERS HATE

STUFF HIPSTERS HATE

A FIELD GUIDE TO THE PASSIONATE OPINIONS OF THE INDIFFERENT

BRENNA EHRLICH
ANDREA BARTZ

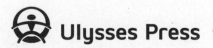 Ulysses Press

Published in the United States by
Ulysses Press
P.O. Box 3440
Berkeley, CA 94703
www.ulyssespress.com

ISBN 978-1-56975-821-2
Library of Congress Control Number 2010925866

Acquisitions Editor: Kelly Reed
Managing Editor: Claire Chun
Editor: Lauren Harrison
Proofreader: Bill Cassell
Production: Judith Metzener
Design: what!design @ whatweb.com
Illustrator: Chris Russo
Cover images: front photograph © Leah Konen;
    background © Chen Ping Hung/Shutterstock.com
Interior photos: see page 223

Printed in the United States by Bang Printing

10 9 8 7 6 5 4 3 2 1

Distributed by Publishers Group West

This book is dedicated to:
EP, Chopper, Jason Schwartzman, Hearst, BT, Ralph Macchio,
PhD, I Hate Everything Hipster, Photog, Leather Jacket,
Tats and all the other cruel, dumb or otherwise misguided
men we've encountered in Brooklyn.
We couldn't have done it without you.

TABLE OF CONTENTS

THE
BEGINNING

[ABSTRACT]

The following study investigates the pressing and urgent question: What is a hipster? Through careful consideration of and immersion in the ethos of the subculture known as "hipsterdom," the authors have gathered a collection of both observations and found documents demonstrating the disposition and character of the modern-day hipster (circa 2010). Results revealed that hipsters are largely negative creatures who gain power and authority by putting things (e.g., music, living situations, apparel, you) down. The authors subsequently conclude that the hipster is more accurately defined by what he or she hates than by what he or she likes.

Keywords:
Subculture
Hipster
Negative
Hate
You

INTRODUCTION

"I know it's not your thing to care/I know it's cool to be so bored."

—Benjamin Scott Folds,
"The Battle of Who Could Care Less"

What is a hipster? The word itself has enjoyed a renaissance of late (early '00s to the present), although it has been in the lexicon for more than 60 years. Merriam-Webster defines the word thusly:

Main Entry: hip·ster
Pronunciation: \'hip-stər\
Function: *noun*
Date: 1940
: a person who is unusually aware of and interested in new and unconventional patterns (as in jazz or fashion)

We, the authors, agree with the above definition. The essence of the hipster is novelty and "unconventional" avenues of thought. Still, the urge to veer off the beaten, primrose-lined path is rooted in one constant, undying urge: to be counter to the culture at large (hence the term "counterculture").

Such an abhorrence of society brewed within the rumbling stomachs of the Lost Generation of the '20s, who took off to Europe to escape the rank atmosphere of American banality (Hemingway didn't call his autobiographical literary odyssey *A Moveable Feast* because he was predicting the advent of fast food). Then came the hipsters of the '50s, best explicated in Norman Mailer's controversial yet frighteningly timeless essay, "The White Negro: Superficial Reflections on the Hipster," in which the journalist describes a group of shiftless elitists uprooted and disillusioned by war and turmoil turning to the fringes of society, embracing utter nihilism and becoming, as Mailer puts it, "philosophical psychopaths." In short: The 1950s hipster consciously shucked off the bounds of society. Sound familiar?

Although Mailer's essay is riddled with antiquated references[1] (and dude uses the term "square" more times than a geometry book), the hipster described in this 1957 work is basically the hipster of today. Forged in a fire fed by hippies (with their languorous nature, disdain for bathing and vehement rejection of their parents), punks (with their tight pants, appropriation and destruction of other cultures, and self-conscious snarls) and grunge kids (with their plaid shirts, sloped shoulders and wretched love lives), the modern hipster fumed angstily in his or her respective enclave, until, fueled by a special form of ennui bred from war, recession and the rise of the Twitter celebrity, they flooded the scene in full force around the end of the aughts.

The mainstream media's initial response: fear and bafflement. *Adbusters* promptly deemed modern hipsters "the end of Western Civilization." *Time* looked askance at their grandma sweaters and affinity for PBR. But soon enough, the term took on a complimentary tone. Fashion writers gushingly applied the moniker to gussied-up *Vogue* editors. Media sources began SEO'ing the hell out of the trendy term, and scores of hipster-themed blogs made their way onto what is playfully called "The Internets." Popular gossip sites such as *Gawker* called for the death of the word not too long after magazines such as *Time Out: New York* shouted for the demise of the concept. Yes, it seems that the age of the hipster—or at least the plaid-clad, Williamsburg-dwelling, indie rock–loving variety—could be drawing to close.

Does that mean that the concept itself is kaput? Well, if the authors believed that, we would have given up this noble pursuit long ago and written a lovely book about how to adopt a kitten or glaze pots—something much less arduous to investigate. Even though superficially the hipster of Mailer's day is no more (the modern-day variety does not, in fact, wear zoot suits and dig jazz), the urge to be everything that society is not will live on. The hipster of the future may not read

---

1 The title itself is obviously rather cringe-worthy.

Bukowski and walk about with a fedora perched on his shaggy head, but you best believe he will probably dislike about 98 percent of the people currently reading this book.

METHOD

Not content to merely observe and blandly comment on the population that we have chosen to study, your humble guides have taken it upon ourselves to infiltrate their society. Bartz likens the undertaking to the invaluable investigations of Jane Goodall; Ehrlich fancies the expedition as fitting into the realm of Hunter S. Thompson's "Gonzo" journalism. Either way, we created this tome via extensive immersion research.

We didn't initially set out to study this intriguing creature; we merely found ourselves interacting with males of the species after moving to New York, where we began wading in the morass known as the hipster dating scene. We were baffled by the backward world our suitors inhabited, since we had just left a structured collegiate environment where beer pong and the Greek system sadly reigned supreme.

After just one year, we had amassed a large enough stable of stories and exes to draw statistically significant conclusions. For Bartz, there was a cadre of artists with an impressive array of side careers: a former American Apparel model/ graphic designer, a neo-Marxist grad student/guitarist and a painter/ falafel chef/pot dealer. Ehrlich, meanwhile, dated what amounted to an entire indie band: lead singer/ guitar player, bassist, drummer and even merch salesman. What did all these men have in common? Besides the innate inability to return a text message or end a relationship in a proper manner, they all possessed a permeating ennui about this thing we call life.

Further exploration into the hipster realm via parties, coffee shops, concerts and jaunts in McCarren Park confirmed that that weary indifference was not limited to the males of the species, but also characterized what the poetically inclined refer to as "the fairer sex." Conversations with hipsters of either gender often centered on topics such as "Why this band is played-out," "How boring this party is," and/or "How all relationships are doomed to fail because life is so crazy right now."

Thus, through the lens of bad dates past, we mused our way to a revelation. We began to see the entire hipster subculture with a discerning eye, recognizing it as a brooding mass of cool-hunters who base their life philosophies on general dislike and self-imposed sadness—i.e., "haters."

RESULTS

By their very nature, hipsters are changeable beasts, chimeras straining against the bars of society's menagerie with the intense and inexhaustible urge to shed one skin and don a more novel persona. While the average body's cells regenerate every seven years, rendering that human (supposedly) an entirely new person, the hipster's process of reincarnation is much quicker.[2]

Other volumes on the subject of hipsters merely describe hipsters superficially, asserting that they wear tight pants, adore flannel and foster a deep, abiding disdain for shaving. But no one culture adheres to a single, immutable uniform,[3] and neither does the hipster. In fact, by the time you're reading this, hipsters may have long shucked off the hallmarks of their current oeuvre, including Keds and a love of infantile games (such as kickball). We, the authors, maintain that this reinvention doesn't detract from the enduring validity of our arguments. Why? Because even as fads flit through the cultural zeitgeist, hipsters will cling to the core belief that everyone else is a loser.

At this juncture, we turn our attention to one of the hipster's most beloved subjects, philosophy, by way of explication: Plato believed that although all people may *appear* to be different—some are thin, some are fat, some are pale, some fake and bake—they are all created from the same mold, the same "idea" that constitutes a human being. One could say the same is true of the hipster: There is a mold out there from

---

2 We are, of course, speaking metaphorically.

3 Except, perhaps, for some religious orders...and our fathers.

which all hipsters are born. And that mold creates people who, regardless of hairstyle or bodily adornment, are identical in that they are defined by what they do not like. What they disdain. What they hate. Therefore, we come at last to the overwhelmingly supported hypothesis of the tract you now hold in your trembling, anticipation-laden hands. Yes, kindest ladies and most esteemed gentlemen: It's cool to be a hater.

Liking someone or something equates a loss of power because it proves said person or thing has penetrated a shell hardened by cigarettes, literature and brooding. Contrariwise, if a hipster hates a band, for example, that instantly alerts those around him that he's better than that band. Likewise, expressing unabashed attention for a member of the opposite sex gives the hottie in question power—if you elevate him/her to the level of romantic importance, he/she can then drop you like a crushed American Spirit, still smoking with extinguished passion. In short, hating is the ultimate shortcut to smug superiority.

The authors have laid out in vivid and captivating detail an accurate and meticulously drawn portrait of your modern hipster. We've included our own field notes as well as a variety of ephemera—pages torn from our subjects' Moleskines, Craigslist Missed Connections, transcribed conversations—and divided them into categories of study (Mating, Grooming, Philosophy & Beliefs, etc.) to better educate you on our elusive subject.[4] We hope that this volume will help you better understand this counterculture. Now, you might want to pour yourself a stiff drink—shit's about to get serious.

---

4 The authors ask that you keep in mind that our study focused on the most extreme specimens of the species. There is indeed a continuum of hipsterdom, and relatively few fall into the all-out hater category. Still, as they exhibit the most amplified embodiment of hipster ethos, we chose to elucidate their behavior as beacons of the subculture.

14

CHAPTER 1

MATING

[CASE STUDY]

Margaret J. is your average hipster girl. She works in publishing, edits a Brooklyn 'zine and, in her spare time, sells vintage clothing on Etsy. Ben Z. is your average hipster boy. He bartends on Tuesdays and Thursdays, shelves books at the independent bookstore on Mondays and Wednesdays, and, in his spare time, practices with his band, Torture My Heart With Your Cruelty. The pair met at a friend's loft party after Margaret spilled her Bud Light Lime all over Ben's raw denim skinny jeans and called herself a "fucking train wreck." After three weeks of "hanging out" (i.e., getting drunk at local watering holes, taking aimless walks at 2 a.m. and consummating their relationship on Ben's air mattress), Ben has ceased to contact Margaret. Consequently, Margaret has begun writing copious amounts of angsty poetry, whilst Ben has penned no fewer than three new guitar licks for his band's first big single (they can "feel it," he says), "I Put the Vacancy Sign up on My Heart."

The hipster dating philosophy is a complicated dance of well-practiced moves (one step forward yields seven steps back), a power battle[5] that ultimately results in one party collapsing from exhaustion while the other matches his/her rhythm to that of a different partner. The key to coming out of the fray unscathed is to cut and run before he/she decides you don't make the cut.

Why the need to turn love into a battlefield? Basically, the self-sabotaging gene is welded into the hipster's DNA. In mythical terms, hipsters are the unicorns—too busy playing in the sunshine to get on the motherfucking ark. While most creatures adhere to the Darwinian drive to maximize the success of their genetic material, the hipsters' mating dance is decidedly less straightforward than others' (see: clean-cut bros shamelessly peacocking[6] to earn a ticket into the female's bed), but, shockingly, no less successful (i.e., they get laid). [See Figure 1.]

---

5 This "power" often falls to hipster men due to the fact that in hipster enclaves such as New York City, Philadelphia and Washington, D.C., single women greatly outnumber single men under 25—and in cities where young, single men are scarce, they tend to play the field, notes 2009 research from the University of Michigan. Moreover, the number of legitimately "attractive" hipster men (read: not "busted-attractive" or "interesting-looking") is even scarcer, according to 2009 research done by the authors.

6 It should be noted that in the realm of hipsterdom, males also "peacock," albeit in less aggressive ways. While a bro may approach a potential mate with an opening line such as, "Have you ever met a professional rugby player before?" a hipster male will demonstrate his superiority/mate quality by quietly pontificating on Ayn Rand.

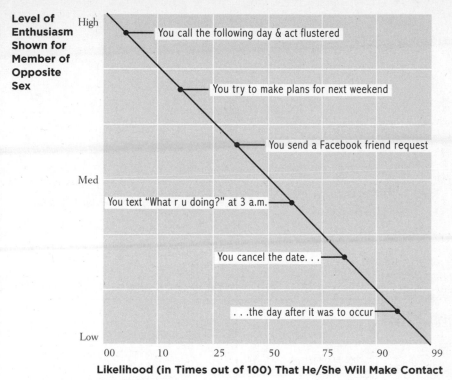

Level of Enthusiasm Shown for Member of Opposite Sex

High — You call the following day & act flustered

You try to make plans for next weekend

You send a Facebook friend request

Med

You text "What r u doing?" at 3 a.m.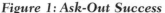

You cancel the date. . .

. . .the day after it was to occur

Low

00   10   25   50   75   90   99

Likelihood (in Times out of 100) That He/She Will Make Contact

Figure 1: Ask-Out Success

Hipster females approach the males, focusing their attention on the tallest and skinniest specimens, pale creatures whose spindly legs barely support their concave chests. The males act aloof, steadfastly refuse to offer the female any form of sustenance and (much like the choosy females of most known species) bypass opportunity after opportunity to mate, delaying copulation until their partner initiates it. And, in the days following roughly the third encounter, one of the pair proceeds to "ghost." If pressed to explain his/her actions, the ghoster cites illness, fear of his/her oh-so-intense emotions or a potent (albeit anachronistic) case of melancholia. In the end, hipsters seek a mate not to bear offspring, but to produce drama, angst and, if they are artistically inclined (as most are), countless albums, paintings and books. [See Figure 2.]

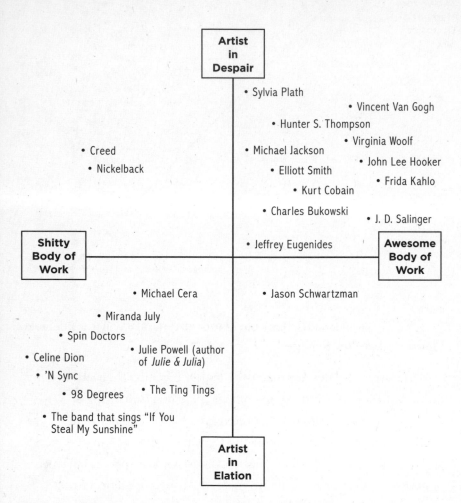

Artist in Despair

• Sylvia Plath

• Vincent Van Gogh

• Hunter S. Thompson

• Virginia Woolf

• Creed

• Michael Jackson

• John Lee Hooker

• Nickelback

• Elliott Smith

• Frida Kahlo

• Kurt Cobain

• Charles Bukowski

• J. D. Salinger

Shitty Body of Work

• Jeffrey Eugenides

Awesome Body of Work

• Michael Cera

• Jason Schwartzman

• Miranda July

• Spin Doctors

• Celine Dion

• Julie Powell (author of *Julie & Julia*)

• 'N Sync

• 98 Degrees

• The Ting Tings

• The band that sings "If You Steal My Sunshine"

Artist in Elation

Figure 2: Quality of Work vs. Artists' Mental Health

ART: Dude, that girl over there is killing me right now.

LARSON: Which one?

ART: The chick with the asymmetrical haircut and the librarian glasses.

LARSON: Which one?

ART: The one in the red romper.

LARSON: Aw, shit, man. She's hot. You should, like, go ask her what she's reading right now or something.

ART: No way, man. I never go up to girls in bars. That's not my style.

LARSON: How do you ever meet girls, then?

ART: They come up to me.

LARSON: No lie?

ART: Yeah. Totally. I figure a lady is only worth my time if she has the stones to hit me up.

LARSON: That's deep, man.

ART: Well, I'm pretty sensitive. I think it's because I'm a Libra.

BUYING YOU A DRINK

The conversation's going well. Filled with scorn for the other patrons of Royal Joke (excuse me, Royal Oak), you lean on the bar and impress him with your knowledge of late '80s post-hardcore punk rock ("Oh, so you guys sort of sound like Fugazi?") and your excellent taste in film ("Yeah, *Clockwork Orange* has been my favorite movie since I was about 14…oh, I know, *Eternal Sunshine of the Spotless Mind* is the most fucking annoying movie ever made.") But despite his intention to bring you home later (a decision he came to, like, an hour ago), dude isn't going to buy you a drink.

He'll conveniently excuse himself to visit the restroom when your whiskey-soda gets low, watching carefully from the shadowy corner so he can return when you've already put away your wallet. Or he'll just continue talking, shooting glances around the bar but refusing to let his eyes rest on your empty Hoegaarden. Unless you're on an actual date, he's as likely to spend money on you as he is to choose "Livin' on a Prayer" on the jukebox. (And let's be honest, if you are on a date you're probably sneaking into a chained-off part of Coney Island at one in the morning, and at best he's kindly letting you take pulls of Jim Beam from his flask.)

Oh, and he probs won't pay for the cab home, either. He may even jump out and strut over to open your door, making like a gentleman while simultaneously leaving you to deal with the blinking meter. This isn't about his complete lack of financial resources. It's because he's a *feminist*. The 21st century is all about equality, babe.

TRADITIONAL FLIRTING

Although hipster boys thrive, subsist and fuel their already horrifically engorged egos (haha, you totally thought I was going to say something else) with that sweet, sweet manna known as praise, a tried-and-true method of snagging an h-boy's interest is a carefully chosen insult. The "neg" is not a new concept (I think that dude Mystery pretty much cornered the market on the little sadistic gem), but using the technique on XYers totally is. You see, the hipster dating scene is a topsy-turvy zone. It's the realm on the other side of the fucking mirror. In short: Hipster dudes are kinda, well, hot girls.

Such girls are wholly secure in their hotness (at least they appear to be), so when someone questions their status as beings of superior nature, they are subsequently intrigued. The same goes for hipster boys. While these "geniuses" appear to be completely confident in their ability to impress their compatriots with their sick keyboarding, lyrical stylings or ability to finger paint like a child, inside, they are basically insecure little boys who—in reality—

couldn't get anywhere near a lady's lips until age 20. Drop a carefully chosen honesty bomb around one of these preening Peter Pans and I guarantee he will be intrigued. You will instantly become: "different," "not a bullshitter" or "real," a litany of adjectives that a hipster boy is constantly seeking in a mate.

If you would like to test out the above concept at your local watering hole this weekend, the authors suggest the following methods:

COMMENTING ON HIS APPAREL

Being a hipster, the man in question will most likely be sporting something ridiculous/unnecessary, making it easy to call him out. However, be careful not to outright insult the dude (i.e., "Does your designated driver roll in a blue bus? Because you look retarded.").

> **Example:**
> **To a dude wearing wayfarers inside—"Why are you wearing sunglasses at night?"**

Such a question is not, by nature, cruel or insulting, but it begs an explanation that will most likely lead to more in-depth conversation:

> **"Oh, I just rolled in from San Francisco six hours ago to promote my sustainable fashion magazine, *Fashion and Fucking*, and I haven't had time to change. Do you like fu- … fashion?"**

CORRECTING HIM OR CALLING HIM OUT ON SOMETHING NONSENSICAL HE SAYS

Hipsters are used to people hanging on their every intellectual word. If you show a dude that you're listening—really listening—to all the stupid bullshit that he's inevitably spouting, he will be intrigued. He will also think you're "smart." Which will be "refreshing" until he realizes that you're probably smarter than him.

> **Example:**
>
> **HIPSTER DUDE:** "I don't know, I guess I just worry sometimes that people think I'm better than them because I'm really quiet and I don't usually say very much. I get really uncomfortable sometimes when I'm, like, in a crowd of people all talking about their art because I can't seem to muster up the *energy* to *comment*, you know? And it's not because I'm not *interested*; it's just that I'm so busy processing what everyone's *saying* and painting mental images of what they're describing that I don't have time to actually put together the words into *sentences* and interject something into the conversation. Because I want to make sure I say the right thing, you know? And not some stupid fucking placating bullshit. I hate that shit. I dunno, I don't really care what people think of me."
>
> **YOU:** "You just completely contradicted yourself."
>
> **HIPSTER DUDE, LATER, TO HIS FRIEND:** "Dude, she just completely called me out. Who is this chick?"

DROP A TRUTH BOMB

The truth hurts, but hipsters love pain. I don't suggest actually bashing a hipster's Etch-a-Sketch installation or telling him in painful detail just how dreadful his poetry slam skills are (no one really enjoys being roasted), but suggesting in some way that you don't quite care will make him seek your approval all the more.

Why? Because, inherently, all hipsters are on a quest for affirmation. If you distinguish yourself from the majority of girls—who often heap on the praise in order to snag the preening peacock—a hipster boy will follow you to the ends of the blighted earth that is Williamsburg. That is, of course, until you finally relent and say something nice. At that point it's Oversville, U.S.A., population: you. And only you.

> Example:
> HIPSTER BOY: "Did you get a chance to listen to my band on MySpace?"
>
> YOU: "No."
>
> HIPSTER BOY: "Oh... That's cool. Some other time, maybe. [Grabs you and starts making out]"

TEXTING YOU BACK IN A TIMELY FASHION

Let us suppose that a hipster girl named Marni is out on the town with a gaggle of other hipsters, kickin' it at a local watering hole's massive experimental jazz dance night. She recently met a hipster boy at her friend's DJ thing at that bar that no one goes to anymore, but she went because, you know, Liam is at least trying to make something of himself (even though he lives in Jersey and gets wasted pretty much every day). For some reason she and this dude with an impressive neck tat started talking. She was struck by his passion for James Joyce and his piercing blue eyes. He was struck by her knowledge of French New Wave films and the fact that she touched his arm a lot. They exchanged digits. They haven't actually gone out yet, but have been volleying back witty texts about the cinematic score of *The Virgin Suicides* and Neck Tat's slight Napoleon complex for days now. It's late. Marni is feeling kind of lonely and blue, so, bolstered by whiskey and against the advice of her friends, she shoots a text to Neck Tat (who is entered in her phone as such, as she does not give romantic interests real names until they earn that right—and they never do).

> To: Neck Tat
> Hey, I'm at Trophy Bar, if you're around.
> Sent: Thurs, Nov 12, 11:45 p.m.

Marni stares at her phone for the next hour and a half. She puts it in her pocket, set to vibrate so that she will know when Neck Tat deigns to answer. She feigns indifference while wondering, frantically, whether she's fucked things up by contacting him as the minutes tick by.

Meanwhile, Neck Tat, sprawled on the floor of his loft, receives and reads the text immediately. He put his phone back on the floor next to the pile of empty Tecate cans and ruminates on what to say. No fucking way is he going to answer after, like, five minutes like some kind of desperate fuck. No.fucking.way. After the requisite hour and a half, he flips open his phone.

> From: Neck Tat
> I'm at home. Come by and hang with me.
> Received: Fri, Nov 13, 1:15 a.m.

Marni, being smashed out of her mind at this point, texts him back immediately, asking what his address is.

Back at Hipster Douchebag headquarters, Neck Tat peeps the text, flips his phone closed, drains a Tecate and settles in for about 30 minutes before the next text. Marni continues to drink.

That's right, children: Although technology has made it possible for us to contact each other in mere seconds, hipsters have devolved the concept of communication, taking us back to the dark ages. You might as well send a fucking telegram, because the average hipster texts at the speed of a carrier pigeon.

When dating a hipster, keep the following in mind:

Hipsters do not want to know anything about you.

Hipsters love mystery and hate anything that detracts from it. Thus, the less you reveal, the better. The following steps have been proven to aid in maintaining total, blissful obfuscation.

1. Upon meeting them, talk only long enough to spark their interest. Abruptly bounce after ten minutes. Don't tell them your last name (so they can't Google you).

2. Turn them down when they first attempt to ask you out. It makes you look like you have a life. Don't tell them why you can't hang—they will wonder: "Does he/she date a lot of people? Is he/she skydiving? Is he/she in prison?" They don't need to know you opted to stay home watching *Weeds* in your underwear whilst shoveling Life cereal into your mouth.

3. Do NOT be their Facebook friend. No one you just met needs to see where you went to school, how many "friends" you have and what you looked like pre-Williamsburg (i.e., wearing collegiate gear while beer-bonging).

4. When you sleep over for the first time (and make sure you go to their place—never let them come over to yours lest they see your embarrassing DVD collection), make your escape before they wake up. Leave a note. Not one that explains where you went, just one that says something to the effect of: "Had to bounce. Text me."

5. Be unavailable for the next two weeks.

DAYTIME DATES

Technically, nary a hipster would actually call a date a date, but for the sake of simplicity we shall henceforth refer to these drunken forays into the tortured realm of romance thusly.

When two hipsters begin the courtship rituals, very rarely will the couple "hang" during daylight hours. Instead, the person charged with "planning" the date will select an establishment that serves alcoholic beverages from a slim repertoire of acceptable watering holes (i.e., ones that are "real" and/or "cheap" and/or "close to my apartment") and casually ask the romantic interest to meet him/her "sometime around 11 p.m. ... midnight ... thereabouts."

The lateness of the hour will ensure a multitude of things:

- **The hipster male will have awoken from his daily disco nap, which is usually taken around 9 p.m.**

- **The hipster female will be in the mood for drinkin'.**

- **The lateness of the hour will prevent the female from getting home in a timely fashion, making it much more likely that she will sleep over.**

- **Consequently, the sexin' will occur.**

Now, let us suppose that this same hipster couple planned a daytime outing to, say, the museum of holography, a local coffee shop or the park. This state of affairs presents a myriad of troubling issues:

- **Neither hipster will likely be awake in time for the scheduled meeting.**

- **The pair will be able to see—in vivid daylight—each and every blemish and imperfection marring the appearance of the other, cracks in the vessel that would otherwise be softened by whiskey and the low light of a bar, loft party or sketchy waterfront park.**

- **Unless day-drinking is to occur, the two will be painfully, unavoidably sober.**

- **Consequently, sex will likely not occur, rendering the entire affair completely and totally pointless.**

In all honesty, hipster dating has little to do with "hearing about your childhood" or "making a connection"—a hipster is often much more absorbed with the "idea" of the other person than the person him- or herself. When one only sees said person under the cloak of night, beneath a fattened harvest moon or dancing in his or her underwear to the Monkees pre-coitus, one can preserve this untarnished idea. When morning comes, each will be merely a dream to the other: pleasant at the time of consummation, but basically forgotten by noon.

"Thanks for the offer, Mr. Chivalry, but I'll pass. Aside from the fact that I don't adhere to the three-square-meals-a-day mores, dinner dates are for Trixies and the 40-year-old I-bankers they met on Match.com (more accurately called 'The Manhattan Meal Plan'). There's the awkward choosing of wine, the sparkling-or-still discussion, the forced conversation between bites of bread, the smiley but uncomfortable, 'Oh, I'm sorry, of course I ask you right as you take a bite,' the holding up of one finger as you furiously chew and swallow so you can respond, the stupid faces that come with biting and masticating, and of course, at some point you fucking flip your knife off the table and onto the floor and make a joke about it but actually want to die.

Better idea: Can we just get sorta wasted, sing 'Stuck in the Middle with You' in that empty karaoke bar and then hold hands (premature intimacy! score!) as we wander along Greenpoint Ave.?"

—Lilly R., 26, caterer and photographer

MAKING THE FIRST MOVE SEXUALLY

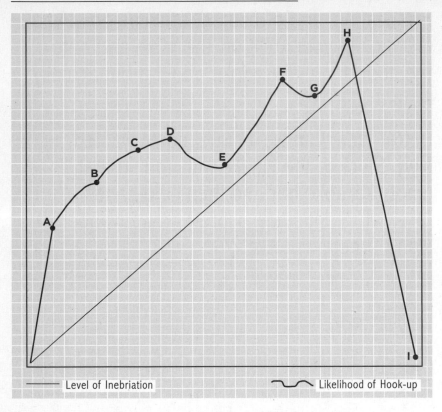

Level of Inebriation | Likelihood of Hook-up

A. He boldly takes you to his roof and shows you the nearby homing pigeons...
B. He gives you an awkward high-five and doesn't let go...
C. You're making out!
D. You continue making out...
E. You continue making out...
F. He touches your hip!
G. You continue making out...
H. He stops. This is it!
I. He passes out.

WAITING FOR YOU TO TAKE HIS PANTS OFF

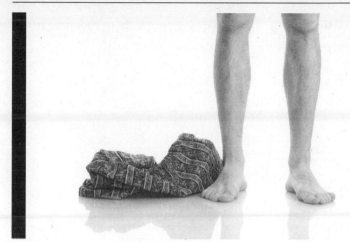

True, hipster dudes love their long, timid mating dance—lingering inches from the chick's face without kissing her, taking her to their bedroom as part of the "tour" without actually stepping near the bed and showing her the collages they made for their now-ex-girlfriend. But all mixed signals and ambiguity fly out the dirty, single-paned window the second she makes the first move and, like, takes off his shirt or bothers running her fingertips anywhere near his crotch.

While bros take great joy in leading a girl's hand to their belt buckle and leaving the whole de-pantsing process to her (*Fucking buttons! Why does your fly have all these fucking buttons!*), hipsters will suddenly stop kissing, sit up and whip off their skinny jeans without a bit of assistance. Maybe they're being helpful. Maybe they're just excited. Maybe they want to make sure it's abundantly clear what will happen next. Or perhaps they're just aware there's no way an outsider could slide off that skintight denim without Vaseline, scissors or about three times the strength of a hipster girl's pencil arms.

MONOGAMY

First rule of hipster mating: Always keep some balls in the air. May we recommend the following romantic interests:

EXHIBIT A: That dude/chick whom you're really into who ghosts for weeks at a time, says he/she doesn't want a relationship and only texts you back at 3 a.m. But he/she will totally come around someday. Right? *Right?*

EXHIBIT B: The dude/chick who texts you every day, whom you're not really that into (at least not physically), but who makes you feel better about yourself because someone wants you.

EXHIBIT C: That dude/chick. The one you met in a bar. For some reason he/she is entered as "Vest" in your phone. Maybe he/she was wearing a vest…

EXHIBIT D: Your best friend.

With this wide variety of romantic interests in play, it's certain: Everyone's getting screwed.

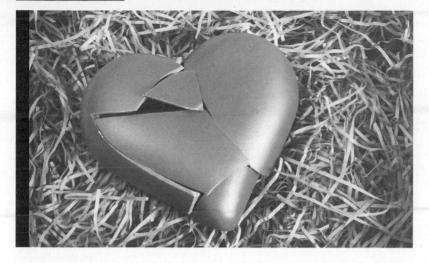

"Yeah, I don't think I want to see you anymore. You don't really need me and I'm kinda intimidated by your real job. I'm not gonna do that whole let's-see-other-people thing though…that leads to all this fucking crying and I end up feeling like a total dick.

Instead I'm gonna just quietly withdraw and stop responding to your texts, occasionally emerging from the ether to send you cryptic, apologetic e-mails about my current bout of episodic depression. I'll use figurative language like 'buried under life' or 'in a cocoon' and make increasingly vague references to hanging out in the near future. Then you'll have a chance to get used to the idea of not having me in your life as I gradually fade into nothingness. (True, one time after I ghosted this chick sent me an e-mail telling me she was all bewildered and furious, but she was crazy possessive or some shit.) That way when I finally run into you at Brooklyn Bowl and I'm with my new girl (the one I started hanging out with when I first sent you those e-mails— chyeah, I dovetail babes), everyone's cool.

Really, this is better for everybody."

—Aaron K., 29, dog groomer and harpsichord player

"Dude, love is so much more meaningful when you're fighting all the time. Love shouldn't be easy—it should be a struggle. Hey, no one ever wrote a timeless, real song about a mutually respectful, emotionally supportive relationship. That's why I date crazy girls/emotionally distant boys who will inevitably leave me broken and wailing into my whiskey, act aloof and unfeeling when stalking new romantic prey, and frequently hook up with my best friends. I take all my relationship cues from books by Bukowski, Murakami and Salinger. Marriage is an illusion. (But I totally wanna get married someday.)"

—Esther J., 24, poet and sandwich maker

CHAPTER 2

SOCIAL HABITS

[CASE STUDY]

Marisol V.'s vintage "Posters of New York City Transit" calendar (a Christmas gift from her clueless mother) has been flipped to September 2008 for several years now. This lack of attention to dates encapsulates Marisol's attitude toward the passage of time. Marisol is a 27-year-old hipster female who works the nightshift at a 24-hour coffee shop, meaning her sleep schedule runs roughly from 9 a.m. until 3 p.m. Consequently, at any given time, she has little awareness of what day it is and is often very pale. She frequently misses prescheduled events such as dinners with friends, drinks with potential suitors and various and sundry medical appointments (all of them long overdue and quite necessary).

Exacerbating this state of affairs is the fact that she, like many of the poor, shiftless souls who make up Gen-Y, has a mild-to-acute case of ADD, meaning she often has trouble committing to any one set of plans. Take last Wednesday night. (Wednesday is one of the few nights Marisol has free.) The previous day, Marisol had asked her friend Jana to accompany her to a party during which attendees would assemble pancakes from a variety of ingredients (Butterfingers, truffles, celery, narcotics). The night of the party, however, Marisol ended up sleeping until 11:30 p.m., at which time her friend Bobbie Lonely called, offering to take her to an ironic disco-themed party at which several C-list celebrities would be in attendance. Marisol, under the impression that it was Monday (her other free night), headed to the party. On the way, she stopped to drink in McCarren Park with a group of friendly looking Crusties, and since her iPhone had run out of juice hours before, she missed the many texts and phone calls from Jana and Bobbie Lonely, the latter of whom sat at home writing anguished poetry about his black, black soul.

With age, most Americans settle into certain schedules: making the morning coffee, showering and dressing for work, commuting, killing one's soul and creative spirit for eight hours a day and then rewarding oneself with either alcohol, food or hours and hours of reality television. And then, when the weekend comes, they rejoice, engaging with relish in preplanned social activities along the lines of bar-hopping, attending a concert or participating in an athletic pursuit of some sort. Not so with the average hipster, who often forsakes societal norms such as "work," "commuting" and "bathing."

Time	Activity
4:00 a.m.	Sleeping.
5:00 a.m.	
6:00 a.m.	
7:00 a.m.	
8:00 a.m.	
9:00 a.m.	
10:00 a.m.	
11:00 a.m.	
12:00 p.m.	
1:00 p.m.	Lying in bed, staring at the ceiling, staving off a crushing wave of depression and a soul-crippling hangover.
2:00 p.m.	
3:00 p.m.	Standing in the kitchen on one leg, eating cereal out of the box.
4:00 p.m.	Smoking on the roof. Watching the pigeons.
5:00 p.m.	Wandering through McCarren Park in hopes of running into a friend or acquaintance.
6:00 p.m.	Working on one's novel in a local coffee shop (i.e. looking at pictures of oneself on Facebook and checking Missed Connections).
7:00 p.m.	
8:00 p.m.	Smoking on the stoop/Forgetting to eat.
9:00 p.m.	
10:00 p.m.	Napping/Beginning to drink.
11:00 p.m.	
12:00 a.m.	Finishing freelance web design project while listening to the latest Brooklyn band on MySpace, feeling intensely envious of said band.
1:00 a.m.	Can't remember. There was probably whiskey. Waking on the F train in Coney Island. The sun is just beginning to rise.
2:00 a.m.	
3:00 a.m.	
4:00 a.m.	
5:00 a.m.	
6:00 a.m.	

Figure 3: A Hipster's Schedule

42

Because this rare species lacks the constraints that shape the social practices of the average Joe Blow American, leisure time is redefined. Instead of being relegated to the weekends and/or the odd "school night," recreation can occur at any moment, punctuating a dreary day like an ethereal ray of golden light in a particularly gloomy cloud formation. Thus, 2 a.m.—considered a late/early hour for most of civilization—becomes a perfectly acceptable juncture at which to board the Bolt bus to Philly to attend a secret concert in a Masonic temple.[7] [See Figure 4.] Scheduling a decent night of drinking and watching cartoons prevents one from engaging in the cornucopia of other activities simultaneously taking place all over the city.[8] Ask any hipster or Kerouacian thinker—the most perfect nights cannot be planned.

---

7 A study in the journal *Child Development* found that most children switch from living in the moment to developing concerns about the future between the ages of 13 and 16, lending further support to our hypothesis that hipsters, much like Peter Pan, are loathe to grow up.

8 Some refer to this anti-commitment credo as FOMO, an acronym for "Fear Of Missing Out." Friends of hipsters, however, refer to it as merely "FO": Fucking Obnoxious.

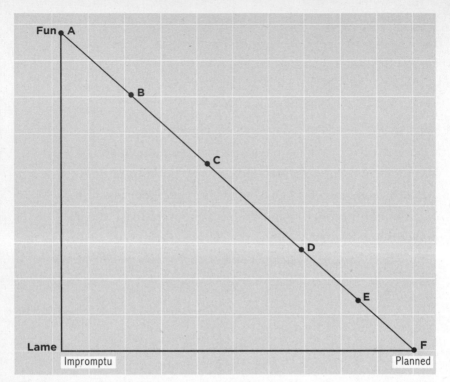

Figure 4: Fun in Relation to Planning

A. Jordan pulls up outside your apartment at 3 a.m. in a borrowed camper with a sentence fragment on his lips: "Mushrooms, seaside, now."

B. Macy texts you at 12 a.m. (while you're already out at a lame bar) to invite you to a rooftop party where a naked dance party later occurs.

C. Johnny calls at 4 p.m. to ask if you want to go to a gallery opening—free wine and snacks (i.e., dinner)!

D. Carla asks you on Friday if you want to see a show on Saturday night. There's a $5 cover and the opening band is kinda OK.

E. Leon e-mails you on Tuesday to see if you want to see his friend's play on Friday night. It's about Bukowski. At least four of your friends from college are in it. You'll have to call the box office to buy tickets.

F. Ernie sends you a Facebook invite—for something that's, like, weeks away—I'm sorry, I stopped paying attention, what's going on?

This joie de vivre has a profound effect on a hipster's interactions with his or her friends, and even the initial selection of this elite group. In order to be tight with a hipster, you must, in a metaphorical sense, bind a blindfold across your bloodshot eyes and let him or her lead you into the dark of the night, trusting that something "fun" will materialize. Hipsters are the Merry Pranksters that Tom Wolfe chronicled in *The Electric Kool-Aid Acid Test*, frolicking children who while away the hours in the darkness of the woods, completely losing track of time until their rumbling stomachs remind them they have not yet supped.

In short: Most of them suffer from an all-consuming affliction known as narcissism, lacking the basic empathy to indulge in the whims of others. Friends function as a means of entertainment and entertainment alone. Once a compadre assumes the faint outline of a real person with "needs" and "desires," the companion loses his or her luster. Thus, if you attempt to plan an evening beforehand, the hipster will retreat, much like a cat when showered with too much attention. Said hipster will say with a casual flick of his head, "I don't do plans," swiftly erasing you from his lexicon of amusement.

ACKNOWLEDGING THAT YOU'VE ALREADY MET

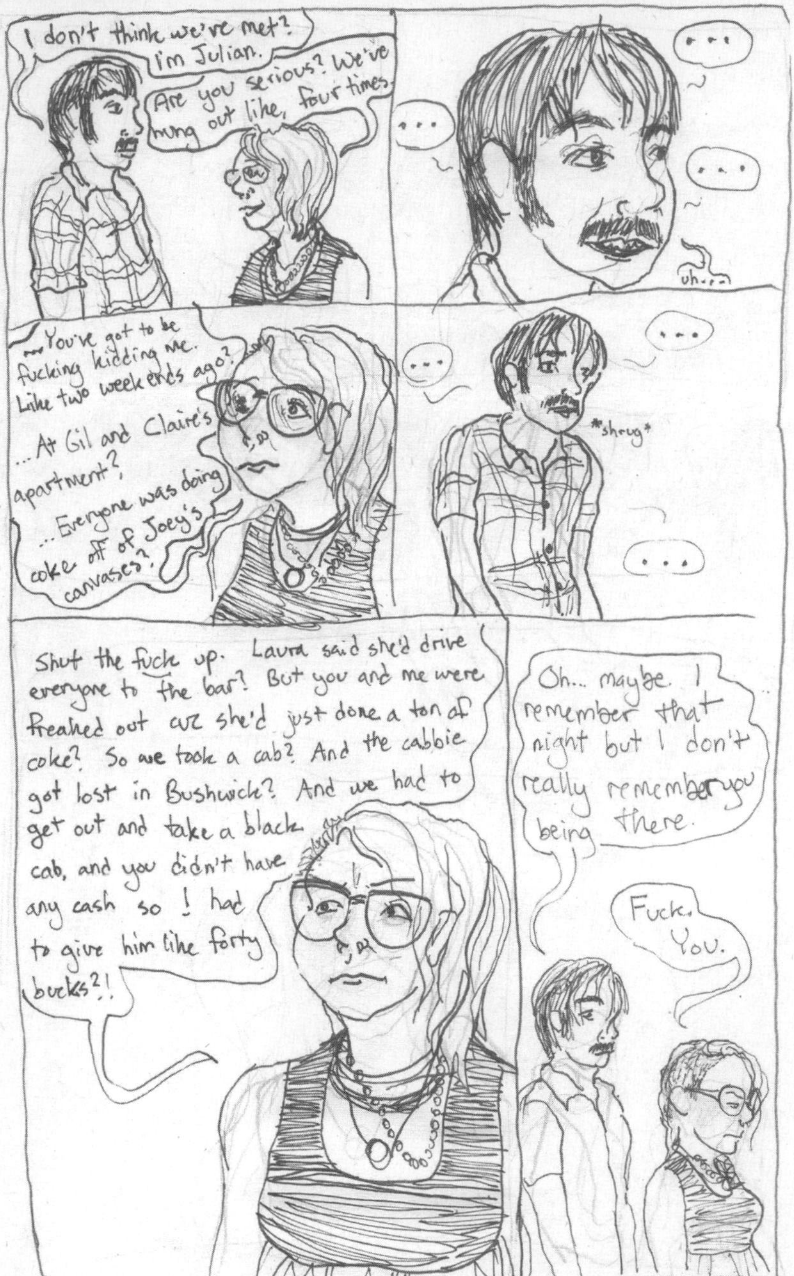

Hipsters love talking about themselves. Ask them a question and they'll answer it in full. Follow up with another query and they'll merrily continue. But they're missing that critical brain structure that compels most people, at some point, to break in with, "…and what about you, how long have you lived in Fort Greene?" Stop asking questions and you'll be met with crickets. At that point, said hipster will sip deeply from his Tecate, gaze around the room and awkwardly slink away.

BEING ON TIME

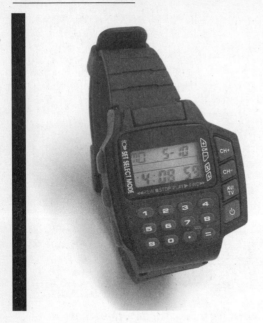

BRIDGET: Dude, you're, like, *so* late! I've been sitting at the bar downing whiskey and Diet Coke and fending off confused bros for the last hour!

SAM: I'm sorry, girl—I fell asleep while reading Hesse on the roof and when I woke up it was all dark and stuff and I couldn't remember what day it was. I was still pretty hungover from day-drinking with Chase and John Boy in McGorlick Park, so I made myself, like, a fucking *huge* omelet and like, 20 pieces of bacon and ate it all at the counter and then Marjorie came over fucking drunk out of her mind and wanted me to go to this dance party with her over in Bed-Stuy and when I said I was busy she broke down and, like, started crying and telling me she *loved* me. So we had to, like, *talk* about it.

BRIDGET: I've been calling you for 30 minutes!

SAM: Oh, my iPhone ran out of power and I can't find my charger.

BRIDGET: That's like the third time you've lost your charger.

SAM: Whatever. Am I really that late? What time is it?

BRIDGET: Dude, you're wearing a watch.

SAM: [looks down at his calculator wristwatch] I don't even know if this thing tells *time*.

"Hey Jen, I haven't seen you since high school. Wow, those are totally sweet flip-flops. It's not lame at *all* that you have the name of your fucking sorority emblazoned all over them (or that you're even wearing flip-flops, for that matter). And that T-shirt is really awesome; everyone *does* love a Tri-Delt, you're totally right. It's not like you wasted a good portion of your college experience parading around in pointy shoes and covering shit in glitter or anything. No. You were making important *social* connections that I'm sure will come in handy when you're looking to round up a group of housewives bored enough to bake cookies for your next book club meeting. I hear the new Mitch Albom is the shit, by the way. I mean, it's not like you were part of some socially alienating collective that requires you to dress, act and think a certain way in order to join. Oh, shit—it was nice catching up, Jen, but I gotta go help my friend Vince set up for this super secret party out in the woods later tonight. Peace."

—Fiona, 23, florist and keytarist

Hipsters know their ABCs: Adderall, Booze, Coke. Knowledge may be power, but the total obliteration of cognizance is totes more fun.

PHOTOS LIKE THIS ONE

A. More than one person is looking into the camera and smiling. If anyone ever notices me skulking around with my Nikon N2000, I take my finger off the shutter, stat.

B. They're at a bar. You can see their fucking drinks on the table (with twists) and the background is a black booth. Really aesthetically pleasing, girls.

C. It's after sunset. Never take pictures after sunset. Flash is for the weak and stupid.

D. That chick is making a fucking gang sign with her bejeweled fingers. Christ, if she knew what that meant…seriously, the only acceptable hand signal for a photo is the lookout (over the eyes). But you're really better off just pretending you have no idea there's a camera nearby.

E. This was obviously taken with a point-and-shoot. The shutter speed is giving me a fucking heart attack. And that is clearly digital zoom.

F. This is probably one of 18 nearly identical photos they put on Facebook in an album entitled "Saturday Night's Alright" or "Big Pimpin' Up in NYC" or "gOoD tImEz <3."

Fuck, somebody fire up the Photoshop so I can make the snaps I took last night look like Polaroids—I need a little fucking authenticity.

HAVING AN ALL-HIPSTER FRIEND GROUP

Yes, 96 percent of the population is not cool enough to be worthy of any given hipster's friendship. But interestingly, a hipster's social circle is not entirely homogeneous. A h-boy or -girl's friend group usually contains, but is not limited to, the following satellites:

The Token Trixie   Any hipster girl worth her Tapatio sauce has at least one made-up, put-together, totally unhipster friend whom she shows off at Bed-Stuy parties and marvels at over coffee—red-eye for Shane, soy chai for Brooke. (Strangely, the hipster half of the pair has no interest in seeing the doll in her natural habitat. In other words, she's happy to trot her fancy friend around Greenpoint like a prize pony on Sunday afternoons, but fuck if she's going anywhere near said friend's favorite Upper East Side bar with its $15 branded T-shirts and mechanical bull.)

The Friend "From Out of Town"
As loathe as they are to admit it, every hipster has a past—a past that most often included a cadre of awkward buds who were similarly really into *The Chronicles of Narnia* and listening to Nick Drake while driving aimlessly around the desolate sprawling suburbs of Middle America, dreaming of the day they'd finally be free from the tyranny of popular Paige and her cronies. Said friend is still a free spirit—she works at the Environmental Protection Agency and lives somewhere kinda cool, like Portland, Maine—but she's not *quite* up on all the trends.

Like, she still reads *The Believer*, and when she visits the hipster ghetto she gapes at all the full-grown men on skateboards and gets super excited when she sees that dude from that band.

That Guy That She Hooks Up with Sometimes Yeah, man, she'll call you at 2 a.m. to come over…but if you want to be included in her brunch plans or lazy weekend picnics, you're S.O.L. Why? I dunno, dude, you're probably the kind of guy who plays "beer games" with his buds at his parent's condo in Vermont, or your pants are too loose. Either way, you're basically a Japanese love pillow: a comforting, kind of weird way to fill a girl's bed, but not to be paraded around in public.

CALLING PEOPLE BY THEIR REAL NAMES

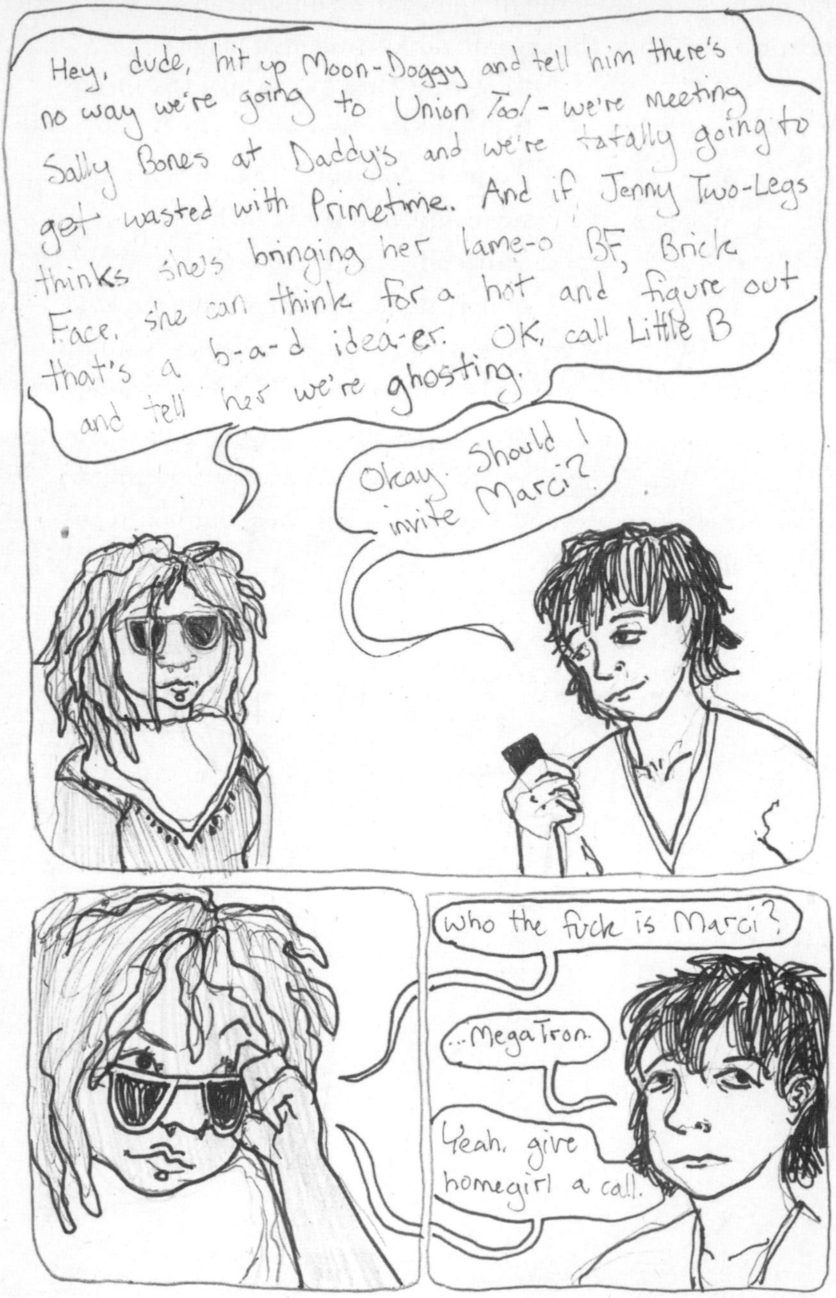

COMING TO YOUR EVENT

R. S. V. P.

BY

M _____

_____ WILL _____ WILL NOT ATTEND

Ha. Yeah, right. That would require:
1. Hanging with your friends.
2. Going to a venue that may or may not be appropriate to visit.
3. Possibly purchasing you a present.
4. Conceivably paying for transport.
5. Foresight.

BRO BARS

The spur-of-the-moment selection of a watering hole is of utmost importance to your average hipster. A bar may be acceptable on one shining Tuesday night, when the beer is flowing like a glorious waterfall of intoxication and everyone is eminently fuckable, and

Ordering a Pitcher: "I didn't even know this place fucking had pitchers. Now, I'm not opposed to sharing, but pitchers connote a kind of chest-pounding camaraderie that makes my pale skin crawl. I can't ruminate on my wasted existence if I have to wait for some slathering bro to allot me my communal mead. Dude, the only time you'll ever see me drinking from a fucking common well is when it's overflowing with liquid hallucinogens."

Trivia Night: "Oh, fuck, who are all these bros and why are they holding slips of paper? Maybe if I have enough whiskey-sodas, the incessant cheering and corny jokes will merely fade into the white noise my liquor-soaked brain makes when I've had one too many. Oh, shit. Look at this slack-jawed, frat-tastic crowd. First Bingo, and now this. The only kind of quiz I wanna take part in when I'm drinking is 'How many fingers am I holding up?'"

completely lame that very same Friday, replete with white hats and sad men from Hell's Kitchen who have decided to "cut loose" in Williamsburg. Still, there are a few constants that render a bar completely unacceptable to frequent.

Fancy Cocktails: "Why in the name of all that is holy is the drink that you are currently clutching in your claws *pink*? I bet you shelled out, what, like 15 large for that sugar-infested, weak-ass beverage, which most likely goes by a moniker best suited to a stripper. I'd much rather earn my epic hangover the hard way—by drinking an entire sixer by my lonesome and then sharing a bottle of whiskey with my lady friend of ambiguous romantic status, who, I can assure you, would never drink anything pink—except maybe that red-flavored Four Loko."

Girls Who Dance Their Way onto the Dance Floor: "I hate you, three girls in bright dresses, looking like popsicles on heels and exchanging the overly excited, "Should we dance?!" nods. Now the three of you, shoulders swaying, hips bobbing, stank faces at full throttle, snake your way through the bar and deep into the crowded dance floor, leaving a sea of swiveling bros' heads in your wake. You couldn't wait 'til you got to the actual fucking dance floor to dance? Am I gonna see you twirling in a cage that floats slowly down from the ceiling like some stupid *Crouching Dragon Hidden Whatever* special effect? Christ. Stephen, let's find a falafel stand and a liquor store and call it a night."

CHAPTER 3

APPAREL

[CASE STUDY]

Lionel S. is a particularly stylin' brand of hipster. As a child, Lionel was mocked for his intense predilection for neon baseball caps and clogs. With eerie prescience, he bucked mall fashions and wore Doc Martens when everyone else was saving up for Nikes. But once he hit his 20s, local girls began fawning over his horn-rimmed glasses and whimsical horse-head belt buckles, and he thanked his lucky stars that when he was a youngster, his mother never bought him the "cool" Tommy Hilfiger shit the rest of the class adored—the gateway (designer) drugs to sure bro-ism.

One sunny day in December of 2008, Lionel visited his local Goodwill, where he purchases the majority of his clothing (with the exception of his raw denim skinny jeans, on which he spends the equivalent of one month's rent). Upon entering the store, he spied a red mechanic's jumpsuit hanging from the wall next to an array of so-ugly-they're-cool Cosby sweaters. Emblazoned across the front pocket was the name

"Ted." Bursting with excitement, Lionel purchased said jumpsuit (for the low, low sum of $6.99), and proceeded to wear it every Wednesday for three months. He referred to the article of clothing simply as "Ted." Girls swooned over Lionel when he was attired in "Ted," and wrote Missed Connections to: "The tattooed dreamboat in a mechanic's jumpsuit who barbacks on Wednesday nights at the Wreck Room. You can give me a tune-up anytime, Buster."

Then, right around the time a sizable hole appeared in the vicinity of "Ted"'s left elbow, jumpsuits began showing up at every flea market and vintage store this side of the East River. Girls wore modified versions known as "jumpers," and everyone was totally loving the ease with which a single article of clothing could be removed before a poorly planned act of drunken copulation. Lionel, however, felt a queer anger growing in the pit of his stomach, so comfortably concealed behind the panel of fabric. As he read Missed Connections every evening, Lionel found it increasingly difficult to discern to which "tattooed dreamboat" they were written. Consequently, Lionel began wearing his beloved "Ted" once a month. By the time Urban Outfitters stocked its first jumper, Lionel had donated "Ted" to the Goodwill from whence it came, and, in its stead, had brought home a particularly gaudy Christmas vest festooned with genuine blinking lights.

While most of America turns to fashion magazines to ascertain the next season's trends, hipsters would sooner die (a wholly unconventional death) than pick up an issue of *Vogue* or *GQ* for stylistic guidance. You're not going to catch a hipster making inspirational collages depicting his or her ideal "power outfit" or "go-to date getup," and hell will pretty much turn into one big-ass skating rink before a hipster takes one of those *Cosmo* quizzes that determines her "personal style." (*If someone needs to take a fucking test to determine whether they're "sporty" or "flirty,"* she'll reason, *she should probably just go ahead and lobotomize herself now.*)

Why the reluctance to turn to Anna Wintour and Tim Gunn for fashion advice? It's not that hipsters aren't into style—on the contrary, they dust off long-forgotten accoutrements and *set* the trends that magazines report on (several months before those fallow fashionistas jump on the bandwagon) and you eventually adopt. You see, the Converse and skinny jeans that most Americans are currently sporting recently adorned the malnourished bod of your average Williamsburg dweller. Take, for example, the hipster uniform du jour: the plaid shirt. This particular fashion has been kicking around since before there was an America to loathe, but hipsters were the latest set to make tartan a must-have for the masses. [See Figure 5.]

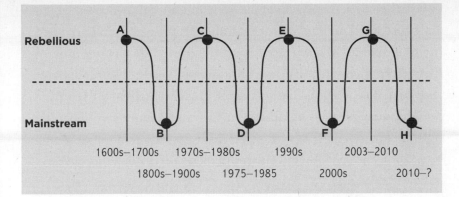

Figure 5: The Plaid Cycle

A. 1600s–1700s: Scottish Highlanders (who saw it as a symbol of self-identification and rebellion)

B. 1800s–1900s: British Upper Crust (who wanted to make like Victoria and Albert and the Duke of Windsor)

C. 1970s–1980s: Punks (who appropriated and bastardized the fabric as a big "fuck you" to the British Upper Crust)

D. 1980s: Preppies (who enjoyed being Anglophiles and feeling refined in their Ralph Lauren)

E. 1990s: Grunge kids (who enjoyed its androgynous nature)

F. 2000s: Copious designers (who got it from musicians/grunge kids)

G. 2000s–2010s: Hipsters (who enjoyed the working man, mountaineer aspect of the look and saw it as a "fuck you" to traditional American society)

H. 2010–?: Tweens (who bought it at Forever 21)

Although hipsters would never admit to willingly setting trends (let alone interacting with the drooling masses on any level), it's almost a game for them: How far will Joe America follow them down the whimsy pit? How wildly can hipsters deviate from the cultural norm before cool hunters and trend archaeologists throw up their hands in bewildered disgust and relegate the entire subculture to the realm of the clinically insane? The answer: pretty fucking far (see: Indian headbands and Harem pants). Like a magic wand, calculated irony transforms ugliness into wearable fashion for hipsters everywhere.

It would be a fallacy to say that a hipster "would never" wear a given article of clothing—mostly because after a requisite amount of time has passed, the article of clothing in question becomes "vintage" and thereby OK to don ironically. In fact, hipsters often delve into the past in order to construct future trends, so flea markets and their parents' closets are prime hunting grounds for hipster apparel.[9] [See Figure 6.] (NB: While scenesters[10] occasionally indulge in the faux-vintage styles of Urban Outfitters and American Apparel,[11] hipsters turn up their bespectacled noses at such lemming-esque behavior.) The secondhand shopping tactic serves dual purposes:

> 1. It ensures that no one else will have the same kitten-emblazoned T-shirt, fuchsia balloon dress or Egyptian-printed muumuu as the hipster shopper in question, because said article of clothing has been discontinued for 20 years, and...

> 2. It satisfies the hipster's urge to always look to the past in search of those glorious "better times" when life was purer and people smoked pot in public and stuff.

---

9 A study in the *Journal of Marketing* notes that most shoppers are less likely to buy a garment when they know it's been touched by another customer—researchers chalk it up to a fear of "cooties." Meanwhile, hipsters, always the mold-breakers, take special joy in breathing in the film and filth from owners past—dust from a more "authentic," moth-bitten era. Call it that "old clothes smell."

10 While people often use the terms "hipster" and "scenester" interchangeably, they are actually quite distinct. According to Merriam-Webster, a scenester is "a person who frequents a social or cultural scene." A scenester doesn't actually live the lifestyle—he/she merely acts as a cultural tourist. Therefore, after dancing wildly at Glasslands with all the longhairs, the scenester cabs it back home, where sweatpants, *Sunny* DVDs and a generously stocked fridge are waiting. The hipster, on the other hand, is "unusually aware of and interested in" every aspect of the scene, such that every moment is spent contemplating "new and unconventional patterns"! Patterns that often involve sneaking onto the bar's patio in the dead of winter, getting too smashed to successfully hail a cab, literally crawling down one's street on one's hands and knees, passing out in the door frame, waking and realizing one has no food to speak of and ruing one's wasted existence. Fuck "frequenting" a scene—a hipster marinates in it. Anything else is just hipster lite.

11 The authors declare no conflict of interest, e.g., investments in the aforementioned clothing stores. But free shit would be cool.

Therefore, although modern hipsters would sooner get into a serious relationship with a law student than wear anything designed by Ed Hardy, in five years or so, bedazzled muscle shirts airbrushed with tigers and vipers could be all the rage. God help us all.

Be on the lookout for these signature pieces:

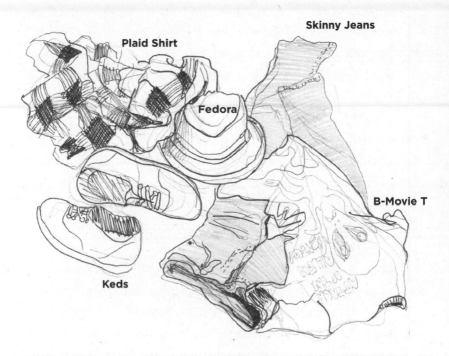

Figure 6: Observations of the Authors with Regard to the Average Hipster Girl/Boy

Headwear: Fedora

    Era: Late 1800s

    Original Wearer: Middle-class men

    Modern-Day Connotation: Used by hipster boys to look "fancy," dapper and gentlemanly—even when one is also wearing paint-encrusted jeans that haven't been washed since the early 1990s.

Top: Vintage B-movie T-shirt under a plaid shirt

Era: B-movie T – '70s; plaid shirt – see page 63, you lazy fucker.

Original Wearer: B-movie T – Nerds; plaid shirt – we repeat the above sentiment.

Modern-Day Connotation: By wearing a B-movie shirt from another era (preferably a top that features a cyberpunk flick) one announces to the world that one is "quirky" and "nerdy," but in a totally cool way. It remains to be seen whether or not the hipster has actually seen the movie he/she is plugging on his/her torso. As for the plaid shirt, Jesus, have you seriously already forgotten the fucking chart?

Bottom: Skinny jeans and white Keds

Era: Skinny jeans – Punk/'50s, à la Grease; Keds – First produced in 1917, Keds were the first sneakers, a word coined to describe how people can "sneak up" on others whilst wearing them (now good for sneaking out the back stairs after a poorly thought-out hook-up).

Original Wearer: Skinny Jeans – Apparently, hipsters stole skinny jeans from the punks, who stole them from '50s rebels, who probably stole them from the local department store; Keds – During our lifetime, they became the preferred footwear of children and that super evangelical Christian girl who wore pleated khakis and wrote Psalms on the chalkboard when you were in high school.

Modern-Day Connotation: Bad boy/girl on top, conservative schoolgirl/boy below. Oh, how hipsters love irony.

DISTINGUISHING BETWEEN DAY- AND EVENING-WEAR

Bros take great joy in transitioning into their going-out clothes—pulling off the ol' polo shirt and cargo shorts, rolling the sleeves of their button-up, looping a smooth leather belt over their khakis, perfecting the collar poppage. Likewise, Trixies can make a whole evening out of ditching the gladiator sandals and pulling on short dresses and heels. (That's actually all they do. They do not accessorize. We cannot figure out why getting ready takes them so fucking long.)

Hipsters, on the other hand, have no real definition of "appropriate attire." For the ladies, white ankle boots that look like ice skates minus the blades plus a vintage sequined mini-dress? A-OK for sitting in the corner of Brooklyn Label, sipping coffee and nursing a hang-yourself-over. A hideous purple sports jersey that looks like it was ripped from the back of a disadvantaged seventh-grader, plus baggy boyfriend jeans and moccasins from your sophomore year of high school? Perfectly acceptable for a night on the town. And hipster dudes basically sleep in whatever the fuck they wore the day before.

Why the uber-easy day-to-evening transition? The explanation is head-smackingly simple: Due to the complete lack of a real job, a regular feeding schedule and a watch that actually tells time, at any given hour, hipsters have no fucking clue what time it is.

SORORITY GIRL

Low-Rise Jeans: Crack is wack. Unless it's, like, a little baggie Xander brought back from his trip to Tijuana.

Going-Out Top: You look like you're wearing the tragic results of setting an eight-year-old girl loose with half of the trimmings aisle at Jo-Ann Fabrics, some satin, and an inexhaustible glue gun.

UGGs: If you're going to swaddle your feet in sheep carcasses, at least participate in a ritual sacrifice.

North Face Jacket: Somewhere out there in the snowy abyss, there is most definitely a factory run by the Masters of the Panhellenic

Universe that churns out identically corn-fed boys and girls, swaddled in moisture-wicking polar fleeces that cost more than a week's worth of booze.

Labeled Designer Clothing: I'm sure you chose it because the LV tessellation makes such a pretty pattern, not because it demonstrates to the world that you use Daddy's credit card for necessities outside newsstand *Glamour*s and yacht club membership dues.

"I'm not really down with any activity that prevents me from wearing a shitload of necklaces, a scarf, a vest and, perhaps, a hat of some sort. So any real form of athletic activity is out, as is actually swimming (rather than running about in the sand), going through airport metal detectors and attending formal functions where elderly family members are present.

I mean, I can dress down sometimes. For example, I'm totally relaxing in bed right now in my underwear. And a necklace. And a cat mask I made out of papier mâché."

—Minerva A., 22, model and book shelver

HEELS

It's extremely rare to encounter a hipster girl in heels—granny boots, yes, stilettos, a resounding, "Hell, no!" Why? Heels imply that you care how you look in a manner that is wholly unacceptable. They epitomize a misogynistic culture that forces women to teeter about like newborn horses—buttocks perky, calves straining and shapely—vying for the attention of a potential mate, a man who will undoubtedly transform said woman into a beaming Stepford Wife. Plus, it's much easier to scale that fence down by the docks and embark on a magical adventure in an abandoned boarded-up factory when you're wearing Vans.

THE ACCEPTABILITY OF JORTS, WHEN WORN BY...

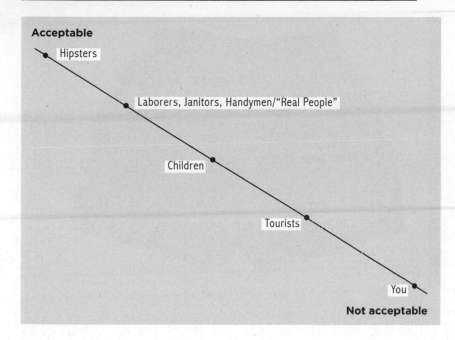

Acceptable

Hipsters

Laborers, Janitors, Handymen/"Real People"

Children

Tourists

You

Not acceptable

BOXERS

"How the hell do dudes get their pants on over those? Oh. They're wearing boot-cut jeans. Or cargo shorts. Yeah."

—Ronald K., 30, freelance animator

WEARING SOCKS WITH SNEAKERS

Doesn't matter that your shoes will end up smelling like the inside of a frat boy's dorm room trash bin one week after purchasing the suckers—you should never wear socks under your footwear of choice. Hipsters wear their blisters like a badge of fucking honor, their fallen arches a testament to their rejection of mainstream, sock-wearing society. If a hipster ever deigned to enter a nail salon, we would pity the poor woman charged with executing a pedicure on those mangled and marinated toes.

WELL-WORN BASEBALL CAPS

You know how you used to break in the bill of a new baseball cap when you were a kid? Lovingly folding the bill and carefully shaping it into a pristine arc? Well, if you want to roll with the hipster crowd, we would suggest you cease and desist with the customization process. Keep the bill straight and set your cap at a jaunty angle and you'll avoid Bro Gap and plummet right into Hipster Douche Cavern.

BRAS

Hipster girls hate wearing them and hipster boys hate when girls wear them. When you're so emaciated that your chest resembles that of a virginal ten-year-old, a bra is just one more piece of expensive fabric that you have to wash and one more article of clothing a hipster dude has to peel off when you're both drunk and skinny-dipping in your heiress BFF's rooftop pool.

CONVERSE

Now, we can already hear the protestations, the torches and pitchforks and cries that we've got it wrong. After all, Converse are one of the most cited hallmarks of the indie set. But after months of extensive immersion research, we are forced to conclude that authentic, through-and-through hipsters hate the ol' All Stars. In major urban areas that double as hipster enclaves, Chucks can now be seen gracing the feet of greasy teenagers, plump, bespectacled 30-year-old women and middle-aged dudes riding the subway to Queens. Hipsters know no loyalty—though Converse have long been beloved by the clique, the trendsetters barely thought twice about kicking their beat-up kicks to the curb the second they noticed white stars gracing the feet of the common man.

Now, they've traded up to equally ratty Keds and Vans (each pair of which, incidentally, they've also "totally had since, like, high school"). To be sure, the childlike footwear will soon spread like wildfire among everyday losers, hot on Chuck Taylors' holey heels, and hipsters will co-opt their next shoe du jour—work boots, maybe, or hip-hop kids' puffy white sneakers. Or mayhaps the hepcats will circle back to the tan Skechers they wore in seventh-grade—exact replicas of the skater shoes that were stolen from the locker room during gym class. Oh shit, Skechers with JNCOs, baby Ts and Y-necklaces as the next It outfit—just call us Nostradamus.

CHAPTER 4

GROOMING

[CASE STUDY]

Jaime K. looks like your average 25-year-old hipster girl: tangled hair, sleepy eyes, pale skin, rumpled clothing. She rarely wears makeup or perfume, and though she showers on a regular basis, she only washes her long, curly hair every week or so. However, Jaime did not always comport herself as such. Jaime attended school in the Midwest, where she would straighten her hair daily and apply bright polish to her shapely nails—in fact, she rarely went out of the house sans a coat of foundation and full face of makeup. She and her friends would frequent local sports bars, where bros would approach her, drawn to her glossy locks and lips. However, Jaime was never attracted to men of this nature, and they were often repelled by her obscure taste in literature and strong opinions about green living. Once, a more freewheeling friend took her to a bar in one of the city's rare pockets of hipsterdom, but the hipster boys there gave her nary a glance, put off by her blush-tinted cheeks and sparkly clutch purse.

Upon moving to Bushwick (the only neighborhood she could afford thanks to her job doing marketing for an Internet start-up), Jaime grew tired of the daily preparations of a "proper lady," which began to feel akin to a virgin cleansing and anointing herself in anticipation of a sacrifice. She retired her straightener, letting her hair return to its natural state, and applied a swipe less makeup every day. A very curious thing happened: Hipster boys began to give her sly glances as she scribbled poetry in her Moleskine at the local coffee shop, and even jangled up to her at her friends' loft parties. Now, Brooklyn locals consider Jaime "sexy." Why? Because she always appears to have just:

a) come home from a trip abroad where acid was in high supply;

b) finished an artistic endeavor of great import; and/or

c) engaged in all-night, coked-out sex with one to three partners.

The idea of embracing practiced disarray is nothing new—fashion magazines have been teaching sexually ambitious tweens to perfect "bed head" for years now, devoting entire spreads to the tousled strands on sleepy-looking models who rub their smoky eyes and/or stretch their sticklike limbs. Hipsters merely take this concept to the extreme, embracing unironed clothing, the natural blemishes and scars of an unadorned face, and the dark eye bags most often seen on claymation characters in Tim Burton films. While hipster fashion is flashy, intricate and attention-grabbing (see Chapter 3), hipsters' grooming rituals take the opposite tack, bordering on nonexistence. As always, outsiders wonder, why the tendency to shun society's standards of beauty? Simple: Because showing that you think about your appearance indicates that you care what those around you think, and hipsters are not having that.

Let us examine each gender independently, starting with the males of the species. Although regular folks may call hipster males "womanly" or "fey" for wearing "their girlfriends' jeans" and occasionally making out with their male roommates, when it comes to grooming, hipster males are far from metrosexual. While males of other leanings take great pains to keep their hair combed and in perfect order, remove unsightly stubble and smell like the inside of a swanky men's fashion magazine, the hipster man is constantly striving to achieve a level of mountain man–esque masculinity: favoring more undone hair styles, allowing his face to darken with a bristly carpet[12] and shunning any bottled pheromones in favor of his own signature smell—grass, sweat and cigarette smoke. Such is the aesthetic favored by men whom the hipster considers "authentic," e.g., drunken authors, janitors and railroad hobos.

By embracing such personas, the hipster male is, in a sense, enacting a kind of rebellion. In most cases, these men grew up privy to a rather privileged existence, never once coming into contact with people like truck drivers, lumberjacks or dock workers. Pre-hipsters were taught to tie their ties before performing with their

---

12 .A survey conducted by Quicken and the American Mustache Institute (yes, really) found that mustachioed men earned, on average, 8.2 percent more than bearded dudes and 4.3 percent more than clean-shaven males. Relatedly, the authors overtip the young Tom Selleck doppelganger who bartends at Clem's.

STUFF HIPSTERS HATE

high school jazz band, to brush their teeth nightly and to keep their hair short and neat. Once they were loosed into the "real" world, where they soon were saddled with service industry jobs and bleak living arrangements, the romance of squalor became more and more appealing. And so they strove to assimilate into the grimy luster of poverty (one fostered by listening to too much Johnny Cash and Neil Young), telling the world that they don't truck with putting on airs. This is how hipster males reclaim their lost masculinity: through five o'clock shadows and scars gleaned from drunken walks home down the back alleys of their youth.[13]

Now let us turn our attention to the hipster female. The reasons for her abandonment of societal norms are rather straightforward. What is a woman taught from Day One? To be charming, lovely, sweet-smelling, graceful and always put together. Since a hipster, by nature, rejects everything that mainstream society elevates, it follows that the hipster female casts off all aspects of femininity that her mother and sisters hold dear. That includes makeup, artificially straightened hair, supportive undergarments and anything else that gives the impression that she is endeavoring to look attractive in the conventional sense.[14]

This divestment of niceties serves dual purposes:

1. The hipster female is demonstrating to the hipster male that she does not, in fact, care what he thinks of her. Therefore, she assumes a kind of power over him (see Chapter 1). Although one would think that meeting a possible sex partner in a state of general

---

13 Sometimes you will come into contact with a hipster who actually did have a hard-knock life. These hipsters are often looked up to by other hipsters, and are, consequently, not really hipsters at all.

14 In this case, we are talking about the majority of hipster girls. There are subsets of hipsterdom—Bettie Page Hipsters, 1960s Beach Blanket Bingo Hipsters, Swing Kid Hipsters, etc.—who wear makeup and the like, but more as an ironic costume than anything else.

disarray would be off-putting, the hipster male is intrigued. The girl suddenly becomes "real," an attribute highly esteemed in the hipster world.

2. By rejecting the traditional feminine attributes—cupid's bow lips, the soft scent of jasmine and shapely leg encased in a haze of nylon—the hipster female embraces her sexuality in a way that borders on masculinity. She revels in her tangled hair, her punched-in eyes and her own natural fragrance. Forget "I feel pretty," a hipster female only strives to feel "powerful."

Again, in the preening habits of hipsters, we see in stark plainness the classic "battle of who could care less." Society may look upon an ungroomed hipster and see a messy child, a gutter punk or a homeless person, but in the realm of hipsterdom, the less you care, the more attractive, strong and authentic you are. Extra props to folks who don't own a hairbrush.

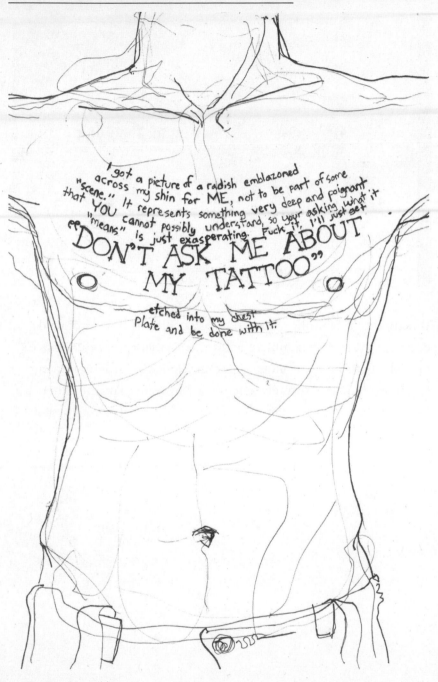

I got a picture of a radish emblazoned across my shin for ME, not to be part of some "scene." It represents something very deep and poignant that YOU cannot possibly understand, so your asking what it "means" is just exasperating. Fuck it, I'll just get "DON'T ASK ME ABOUT MY TATTOO" etched into my chest plate and be done with it.

WASHING THEIR HAIR

Whether it's a carefully arranged angular coiffure, a mess of wild curls or a Jesus mop complete with a beard that sprouts along one's face like moss creeping along the forest floor, the structural integrity of a hipster's hair is severely jeopardized by water. Forget "lather, rinse, repeat"—hipster hair-washing comes at regular, widely spaced intervals, like the wax and wane of the full moon.

STUFF HIPSTERS HATE

Hipster, why are you so white? I see you frolicking in the summer sunshine through every outdoor craft fair and ironic family-fiesta-themed cookout (with balloons! balloon-es!) this side of the East River. Yet your skin is as white as fresh milk. Are you sneaking on 50+ SPF, showing foresight and concern for your health in the most unhipsterish manner? For shame.

BEING CONVENTIONALLY ATTRACTIVE

In the hipster world, being hot is a lot less important than being "interesting looking." While a dude with close-cropped hair, a chiseled jaw and a swimmer's physique may be a prime physical specimen to the rest of society, to a hipster he's pretty much a nonentity. Let us suppose that people only really take note of the members of the opposite sex that they find attractive, rendering the rest of society invisible: When a hipster walks into, say, Abercrombie & Fitch, it is as if she is walking into a room bereft of humanity, filled only with douchey clothing. In order to make oneself visible, and therefore sexually viable to a hipster girl, one must find a way in which to distinguish oneself from the cellophane crowd.

Really, it's simple mathematics:

Take one attractive man and add one (or all) of the following:

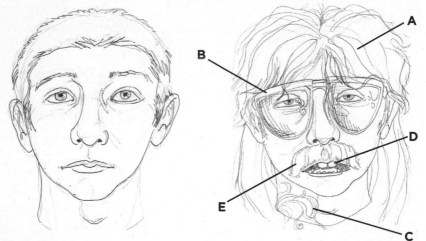

A. A mullet
B. Oversized "nerd" glasses
C. A coloring book of half-finished tattoos[15]
D. Fucked-up orthodontia (there's a reason Death Cab For Cutie has a whole fucking song called "Crooked Teeth")
E. An anachronistic 'stache.

15 Warning: This method can backfire if you are too clean-cut, making you look like a fireman or a cop.

STUFF HIPSTERS HATE

And what do you get? Tragically marred beauty. And there's nothing hipsters love more than tragedy.

NB: This method can also save outright ugly dudes from living the celibate life. It's amazing what a well-placed tat and some camouflaging facial hair can do for a guy who would otherwise be spending his Saturday nights watching *My So-Called Life* next to a box of tissues…for the tears….

"Spending $80 to have my hair cut and blow-dried at a salon? Fuck that. My awesome friend Steven Gherkins (stylist and local GOD) (you'll meet him someday) does it for me for free on a lawn chair on Jillian's fire escape. Only he can sculpt my perfectly asymmetrical mussed 'do (or, alternatively, WWII-inspired pompadour). I repay him in cigarettes and Jim Beam."

—Donald G., 28, art assistant at a modeling agency

(Authors' note: Hipster girls let their split-end'ed hair grow to their waist. Their bangs they trim at home with rusty scissors over the bathroom sink.)

MISSED CONNECTION: You were wearing Axe body spray – w4m (Lower East Side)

Date: 2010-08-07, 6:59PM EDT

Reply To This Post

Oh, my. What is that undeniably sexy smell? All of a sudden I have the intense urge to tear off all of my clothes and rub myself all over you, dude in the black button-up shirt who has indulged in copious amounts of hair gel. I can hardly tell that you purchased your fragrance of choice at the local Rite Aid, most likely along with a sixer of Bud and yet another economy-sized box of condoms (it's sad when those suckers expire, isn't it, dude?). My nose is not at all burning with the slightly acrid scent emanating from your furred chest—and it's kind of awesome that I can smell you all the way over on the other side of this subway car, where I am currently huddled, sneezing. And the fact that, even after I have exited this train, leaving you to wend your merry way to Midtown, your manufactured man musk will linger in my nasal cavity only makes me want you more. Still, I know it is not to be—your intense manliness is just too much for me. Until I can gather up the moxie to make you mine, I believe I will persist in pursuing soft, pale dudes who revel in the smell of their own rumpled bed. It's probably better this way. Good luck breaking in those 'doms, man.

• it's NOT ok to contact this poster with services or other commercial interests

PostingID: 1633299878

BODY GLITTER/SHIMMER

Now, let's be clear—face paint, which sometimes sparkles, is acceptable. The Kevin Barnes look, while woefully outdated, is not an actual object of hatred in the hipster community (more a subject of apathy). However, body glitter and, more commonly, "body shimmer" (often found in powder or lotion form) are utterly abhorrent. The aesthetic that one sweats glitter, that one naturally possesses a metallic sheen, is, quite simply, stupid. Women are not Pussy Galore on her gold-plated deathbed. They aren't Twilightian vampires, twinkling in the sunlight like human-shaped disco balls or those Elmer's glue–based homemade ornaments. True, hipsters will gladly deck themselves out in various metals, plastics and other shiny baubles in the form of jewelry, headgear and bling. But their milky white skin is no home for specks of sparkle.

At its most basic level, right there in its DNA, glitter is viral, infecting one part of your body, spreading to your face and hands, and then replicating itself on unsuspecting bodies around you. It's basically metallic herpes, and hipsters don't need any more of *that*.

THE DENTIST

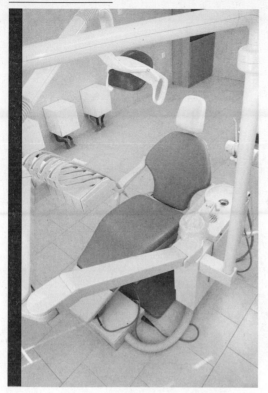

For starters, the proportion of hipsters with creative teeth spacing is higher than in the general population. (The same parents who name their son "Arthur" are a bit less likely to see braces as a necessity.) Further, hipsters are all, "I haven't been to a dentist in, like, three years." Why? Well, they've been too busy taking pictures of one another strumming on six-strings and strewing empty beer bottles strategically across their hardwood floors (you know, for effect). Also, it's hard to pencil in that annual cleaning when you don't have health insurance.

MUSCULATURE

Allow us to introduce you to a little concept we like to call "hipster soft." Although your average hipster has been blessed (by either nature or the nicotine gods) with a slender frame, many lack what fitness magazines refer to as "muscle tone." So even though a hipster male may have a broad (albeit sunken) chest and slender waist, just give his midsection a poke—Pillsbury Dough Boy–style—and it'll bounce right back at ya like the proverbial bowl of jelly.

It's not that said hipster overindulges. The fleshy expanse is not even the gentle swell of a burgeoning potbelly.[16] It's just that

---

16 Shut up, *New York Times.*

the concept of strengthening one's core is as foreign to a hipster as his favorite obscure dance film is to everyone else. While a hipster may have marginally toned arms (from playing various musical instruments) and slightly defined calves (biking 20 miles in the snow will do that to you), he will never have the cut physique of, say, one of *Cosmo*'s 50 most eligible bachelors. That would require sit-ups, and just sitting up is hard enough when you need to drink yourself to sleep in order to make it through those long, cold Brooklyn nights.

"Who the fuck uses hair gel? That neon-colored shit with the little bubbles suspended in it? Do you really think I would walk into a bodega and buy myself a bottle of L.A. Looks or whatever the fuck that is? My signature coif is all ozone, Parliament ash and natural musk, thank you very much. (And a little bit of overpriced styling paste. But that's between me and God.)"

—Randy K., 25, foot messenger and drummer

MANICURES

RHODA: I wanna day-drink and you're coming with. Let's get an early start, so that means you have to be up by, like, three.

RENEE: I'll be up. I think I'm gonna try and get my nails done that morning.

RHODA: Jesus, you get manicures? I've never gotten one.

RENEE: Oh, I love them! I go to this little place in the East Village, I always have this really sweet Vietnamese lady.

RHODA: The whole concept is so weird to me. Isn't it awkward? Sitting there while this immigrant who barely speaks English slaves over your nails?

RENEE: Why would it be weird? It's like, her job.

RHODA: That's fucked up! Think about it, the woman is actually *washing rich women's feet* like fucking Mary Magdalene fussing over Jesus' gnarly sandaled heels.

RENEE: Whoa, wasn't comparing myself to the anointed one, I just like having my fingers French-tipped.

RHODA: And do you know how freaking *bad* that shit is for the environment? Fucking killer to all the little dog babies and cat babies they undoubtedly test that glitter-encrusted Princess Crème Puff Pink bottle of evil on.

RENEE: Don't be a hypocrite, dude. I mean, you have nail polish on, too!

RHODA: What? No I don't!

RENEE: I'm mean, I have no fucking idea why you would choose a clear yellow polish, but I can totally see it. Don't front.

RHODA: Dude, this is the way my nails *look*. I guess it's from smoking so many rollies....

RENEE: Uh-huh…

RHODA: Fuck you. At least I don't murder puppies by proxy.

RE-UPPING ON TOILETRIES

Soap and shampoo and whatnot cost money, and acquiring them involves the unbelievable hassle of, like, going to the store. Therefore, a hipster will attempt to postpone the process of toiletry shopping for as long as possible.

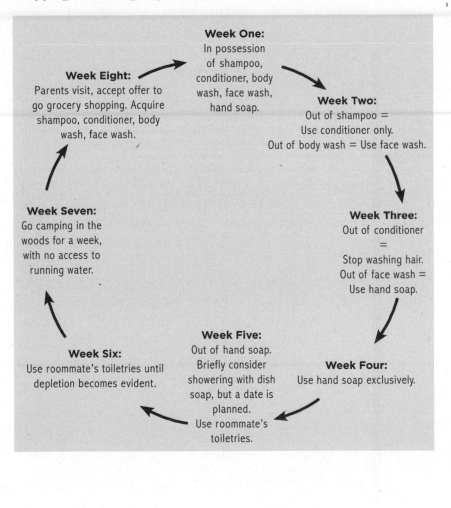

Week One:
In possession of shampoo, conditioner, body wash, face wash, hand soap.

Week Two:
Out of shampoo = Use conditioner only.
Out of body wash = Use face wash.

Week Three:
Out of conditioner =
Stop washing hair.
Out of face wash = Use hand soap.

Week Four:
Use hand soap exclusively.

Week Five:
Out of hand soap. Briefly consider showering with dish soap, but a date is planned.
Use roommate's toiletries.

Week Six:
Use roommate's toiletries until depletion becomes evident.

Week Seven:
Go camping in the woods for a week, with no access to running water.

Week Eight:
Parents visit, accept offer to go grocery shopping. Acquire shampoo, conditioner, body wash, face wash.

CHAPTER 5

HABITAT

[CASE STUDY]

Shirley C. moved to Brooklyn a bright-eyed Midwestern girl with ardent dreams of opening her own gallery/coffee shop/Laundromat, for which she had already come up with the perfect name: "Spin (Life) Cycle—where both the wireless and creative spirit are free-flowing." Although she knew to a certain degree that NYC's cost of living is higher than that of, say, Mount Carroll, Illinois, she also knew that if she was to survive her anguished mid-to-late 20s she would have to move to a town where there were more eligible and enticing mates than that 27-year-old, semiracist legal aid with a gun rack and an unironic passion for taxidermy.

During her first year in Brooklyn, Shirley shelled out $1,500 a month for a room in Park Slope—on her parents' dime, naturally—that lacked a proper door and was often visited (sans invitation) by a stray cat who prowled her fire escape during the night and who also had a time-share with the rats in the garbage can downstairs. Hence, Shirley lovingly called the stray "Garbage Cat." By year two, Shirley's trust funds were dwindling, as was her parents' patience with her "artistic lifestyle" (since she hadn't quite opened her own coffee shop so much as landed a job in one). Weary of stroller-dodging in the Slope, she scouted out an apartment in Bushwick. She now lives with two Craigslist-found roommates both named Matthew (one of whom she sleeps with when she's drunk) in a lofted space legally intended to be used as storage. The apartment is located above a funeral home and smells of formaldehyde whenever the outside temperature tops 45 degrees.

For most of the country, that old adage "a man's home is his castle" rings oh-so-true. Even after racking up a few years of partying ("Hey, even Mom and Dad were crazy back in the day, amirite?"), a typical citizen settles down and focuses on that ultimate life goal of having a mortgage, a roof over his head, top-notch vinyl siding, a backyard swing, a mailbox with his name on it, neighbors to whom to present fruitcakes—in short, home sweet home. Not so for your average hipster. For one, she lacks the funds and foresight to occupy a truly stellar abode, and, two, living in squalor is just more romantic.

Let's begin by painting a vivid picture of the average hipster's neighborhood, which is most often a not-yet-fully gentrified locale, i.e., it remains "real." In New York, those districts include far-flung spots in Brooklyn such as Bushwick or Bed-Stuy. You know how in *A Tree Grows in Brooklyn*, the immigrant grandmother character is all about owning land as a way of cementing her place as a true-blue American? Times have changed. Although those immigrants are still living in Brooklyn (in cultural enclaves that they admirably, steadfastly occupy despite the chilling tides of cultural annihilation), they now share the sidewalks and city blocks with a bunch of weirdly clothed arty kids who roam the streets at all hours of the night, peeing on cars and sounding their barbaric yelps to the rooftops. In a sense, hipsters seek out these locales as a way of existing on the margins, living amongst those who have not been truly, fully assimilated into the apple-pie-flavored, BBQ-smoke-laced, morbidly obese American Dream.

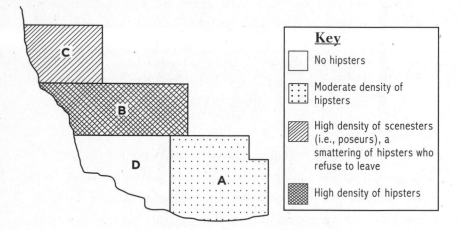

Figure 7: Hipster Density Map

A. A neighborhood with a Polish bar where only locals hang, one bodega and a taco restaurant.

B. A neighborhood with a Polish bar where locals hang early in the evening (leaving it open for late-night revelry), three bodegas (one with a selection of organic food, one with an array of breakfast cereals and one with soap and stuff), a liquor store and a used bookstore with an amiable bookshop cat.

C. A neighborhood where there's a central street replete with bars, cafés, bookstores, record shops, boutiques and a single New York Muffin.

D. Anywhere with a Borders.

In addition, these areas often have a relatively low real estate value, as they are located off of undesirable train lines and are regularly featured in the local police blotter. Consequently, apartments are often on the "rustic" side, lacking amenities such as functional bathtub drains, proper heating and cooling systems, and bathroom sinks. However, they do boast mice, roaches and superintendents who make their pocket money via an S&M dungeon run out of the basement of their tenants' building. While these living situations are far from ideal, the hipster lacks the capital to secure anything better, and seeing as how she most likely labors in an artistic field that renders her completely unable to retain excess funds (*Hey, a girl's gotta drink—er, paint…*), she will never be able to stow away enough cash to relocate to a more domesticated living space.

And, secretly, she'd rather not. Such dilapidated dwellings serve a triple purpose in a hipster's life: They save her money, lend her indie cred and provide her with endless stories to tell friends and future lovers ("Dude. My apartment is fucking haunted. You would not believe the shit that goes down here. I swear I live in the freaking Dolphin Hotel.").

Sadly, as more and more of the hipster set occupies such neighborhoods, all vestiges of the once ethnically diverse community are eventually blotted out: the Ukrainian bakeries become ironic bars, the grocery marts all-vegan cafes for rabid locavores. Eventually, said 'hood becomes what's known as a "scene."[17] Cue the influx of bros and Trixies, comforted by the presence of that most hated of establishments, Starbucks.[18] When the mermaid seal

---

17 This is defined as the *consumption-side* theory of urban gentrification, wherein the sociocultural traits of the gentrifiers drive the process. A "new middle class" comprising artists and cultural leaders moves into an area, serving as the first-stage gentrifiers, making it habitable for the second wave. Still, the authors caution against calling a hipster "middle class"—crying and yelling will likely ensue.

18 In *Everything but the Coffee: Learning about America from Starbucks*, Temple University scholar Bryant Simon claims that the chain's initial success elucidates Americans' quest for meaning, community, justice and relevance in the 21st century—via consumerism. At its peak, S'Bux demonstrated how much time, energy and emotion people are willing to invest into what they buy, as a representation of who they are. (To a hipster, of course, most Americans are as fat-laden, repugnant and pumped full of artificial sweeteners as a Venti Mocha Frappuccino Blended Coffee Light with Extra Whipped Cream.)

arrives, your average hipster will pack up her plywood loft room and relocate to the newest "real" neighborhood—one where people still have lawn ornaments and shit.

Although your average hipster thrives on being "quirky," "unique" and—to the majority of society—"fucking weird," no one wants to exist in a neighborhood in which you find yourself perched at the very top of the out-there totem pole. So, while one may have mild celebrity status as "The Literal Williamsburg Hipster Dude" (the homeboy who rocks 17th-century garb whilst strolling down Bedford on sunny days), "Awesome Mustache Man" (that guy with the

epically waxed 'stache whom you see at the bus stop every morning) or "Squirrel Tail Chick" (the girl who sells and wears animal tails at the flea market), one finds comfort in living in a 'hood chock-full of true-blood local personalities, such as "Dude Who Bikes Around the 'Hood Singing 'La Bamba,'" "Lady with Small Dog Perched on Her Shoulder" and "Naked Unicyclist."

These unflappable luminaries are a testament to the creative joie de vivre of one's cultural enclave—a gay reminder on grim days that there are people out there living their merrily-we-roll-along lives to the fullest, all day, every day. Nary a hipster will actually speak to these vivacious victors of the grayest afternoons; to do so would shatter the illusion and render said icons mere beings of flesh, bone and pulsing blood.

That and they're all probs legit insane.

MARTIN: Oh man, I was just on the fucking Chinatown bus for, like, four hours. It smelled like pancakes the whole time.

SEAMUS: Did you go to Philly?

MARTIN: Naw, man. Boston. My friend lives in Allston and I haven't seen him since he got back from hopping freighters for the last six months. He had some crazy stories—fell in love with some punk chick from Toledo and he's getting together the money to build a cabin for her up in the wilds of who-the-fuck-knows-where, Ohio. Keeps talking about how he's gonna bust outta Boston, get his tats removed and open a taxidermy studio up in O-ville. He's livin' his life, man.

SEAMUS: Yeah, but, dude. He lives in Boston? I fucking hate Boston. Fucking Freedom Trail my ass…

MARTIN: Yeah, man. It's kinda awful. He kept telling me that Allston was, like, the Williamsburg of Boston. But, dude, all I saw were these fucking college kids everywhere, and these terrible sports bars filled with total fucking poseurs with tribal tattoos and surface piercings.

SEAMUS: Yeah. All my friends who go to art school live there. I guess there's supposed to be a scene somewhere.

MARTIN: But, dude, get this. I was on the train and there was—I swear to God—a throng of frat-holes in fucking suits and sunglasses fighting about who was gonna get sexiled that night. Like, one dude was seriously gonna cry. It was like the terrible, terrible college experience I never had.

SEAMUS: Well, that sucks, dude. Let's go get a drink, wash the Chinatown bus stink away.

MARTIN: Yeah, if you're buying. Where?

SEASMUS: Matchless?

MARTIN: Naw, that place is Dante-esque now. The white hats were out in force last Tuesday.

SEAMUS: OK, the Levee?

MARTIN: Are you fucking kidding me? Dude, that place is like a halfway home for old weird dudes who still think they can get laid.

SEAMUS: The Charleston?

MARTIN: Now you're just being stupid.

SEAMUS: Ah, man, I don't know then. What do you want to do?

MARTIN: Ah, fuck Williamsburg. Let's borrow Pedro's car and drive to Chicago. I hear Pilsen is OK now.

FAMILY NEIGHBORHOODS

STROLLERS

"Urine-soaked chariots used to transport screaming wretches down an already congested sidewalk with undue speed. The fact that your child is contained in a bubble of plastic does not negate its existence. Please remove said apparatus from *my* neighborhood."

BABY HIPSTERS

"Although you are cleverly disguised so as to look 'hip,' what with your tiny Replacements T-shirt and artistically disheveled hairdo, I recognize you for what you are: a wailing, whimpering, slightly damp excuse for a human being. Yes, your parents may be attractive in an I'm-way-too-fucking-old-to-live-in-Williamsburg-but-I'm-gonna-rock-this-sleeve-tat-anyway kind of way, but their tragically fading hotness is not enough to overshadow the horror that is you."

CHILDREN

"Am I near a fucking elementary school? Children freak the shit out of me. They wear mismatched clothing, eat unbalanced meals, dance wildly, demand the spotlight and like, bawl or mope when things don't go their way. They're like less articulate versions of my friends."

STARBUCKS

MISSED CONNECTION: I love the way you describe the loose tea varieties – m4w – 25 (Brooklyn Label, Greenpoint)

Date: 2010-03-16, 5:40PM EDT

Reply To This Post

Yeah, I hate Starbucks because of that whole corporate, fuck-the-man song and dance (and because their coffee tastes like the inside of a garbage bag), but there's a deeper reason for my abhorrence of the frappe-hawking chain: the absence of you, my ethereal coffee girl. O beautiful angel with a septum piercing, you provide the perfect remedy for a Wednesday morning hangover in the form of a cup of deep, black Joe and a half smile. True, I hardly ever talk to you, aside from an occasional "thank you" and perhaps a comment about how tired I am. I merely slump at the counter, pretending to read Howl while sneaking glances in silent desperation. Starbucks just doesn't afford as many opportunities for unrequited love—maybe because no one looks hot in a green apron and baseball cap.

• it's NOT ok to contact this poster with services or other commercial interests

PostingID: 1634699821

THE BRANDING OF BROOKLYN

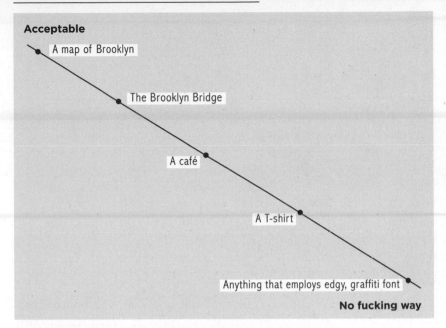

The Acceptability of Emblazoning Something with the Word "Brooklyn"

Although hipsters claim to hate where they live, they are fiercely protective of their borough, which is why you will NEVER see a hipster sporting any article of clothing emblazoned with the word "Brooklyn." Especially since such things are often designed to look super "urban"—what with funky splashes of paint and silhouettes of the BK bridge, and, worst of all, exclamation points. And, to add insult to injury, Brooklyn apparel is often found encasing the bulging bodies of NYC tourists, people who—in the average hipster's opinion—have no right to even set *foot* on Bedford. Still, ironically enough, hipsters often don shirts carrying the names of said tourists' hometowns and even, sometimes, said tourists' high school baseball teams.

REMAINING IN ONE PLACE FOR TOO LONG

ASTRID: Oh, man—I gotta get the fuck outta Dodge. The oppressive air of this teeming metropolis is really starting to wear the treads of my soul thin.

JOAN: Oh, yeah. I know. Yesterday the bus driver yelled at me because I fell asleep listening to that really chill Low album and I ended up back at the fucking bus yard or wherever the fuck buses come from.

ASTRID: That's nothing, dude. I was picking up my CSA downtown and was like, struggling down the street trying not to, like, drop sprouts and shit all over the sidewalk and my skirt split in the back and the whole fucking street got a real good look at my red underoos. Did anyone stop to help me? No. And that was a fucking brand-new skirt. I bought it at Salvation Army last week.

JOAN: We should take a trip this weekend or something, you know, get away from all this fucking concrete and see something new.

ASTRID: I know. I think we should go out to, like, fucking Berlin or something. Live in a squat and smoke foreign cigarettes and cook beans over a Bunsen burner, shoveling them onto crusty stale bread to satiate our hunger after hours of traipsing across the blighted city.

JOAN: Oh, I was thinking we could borrow Mark's car and drive to Portland. Dean's marching band is playing a protest this weekend.

ASTRID: That works.

Let's take a quick jaunt around your suburb's sparkling beacon of hipsters' three least favorite C's: Commercialization, Capitalism and Crate & Barrel. Past the huge marble slab boasting the complex's pompous yet nature-based name (Beechwood Square, Old Orchard, Stonestown Galleria) is a veritable palace of glass and chrome, fluorescent lights, price tags, poseurs and screaming children. Note the pimply teenagers, hanging in packs and sulking into their Orange Juliuses. Take in the overweight women in sweatpants arguing over the price of an additional tub of frosting at the Cinnabon counter. Coast past the Abercrombie, with its boar head, awful blasted frat music and stench of cologne. Avoid the food-splattered six-year-olds screeching and tearing from the toy store to the candy store for refueling. Spot the painfully unattractive middle-schoolers fondling earrings and cheap baubles in Claire's. Narrowly avoid the kiosk douchebags yelling accusatory questions about your cell phone like creepy catcallers in Spanish Harlem. And take a pause here, brave traveler, in front of Hot Topic. This, my friend, is why hipsters hate the mall.

"It's not just because the fucking jackhammer wakes me up at 11:30 a.m. when I'm desperately trying to recover from last night's epic whiskey-and-cocaine bender, or because the construction workers (who woke up around the time I was trying to pass out in the general vicinity of my bed) persist in yelling shit at me like, 'Hey! Puss in boots!' when I'm kickin' it out of my building in the morning in my holey short-jorts and Fryes. It's because of what the work zones *represent*—the complete and total consumption of the dying earth by bricks, steel, mortar and Formica counters. Looming towers of corporate evil casting the tenements of old in the shadowy chill of a cultural whitewash. It's all a whited sepulcher, man. A whited fucking sepulcher. All the palimpsest in the world ain't gonna create nothing but a city that is intrinsically designed to crumble into the sea. But, yeah, mostly it's because it's *so fucking loud*. I need, like, industrial strength Vicodin to snooze through that bullshit."

—Stella G., 24, restaurant hostess and fiction writer

Doesn't matter if they live in Brooklyn. Doesn't matter if they live in Iowa. Hipsters hate where they live for one of two reasons:

a) There are too many hipsters, or

b) There are not enough hipsters.

Unlike Goldilocks, they can never get the porridge *just right*.

Therefore, even the hippest of hipsters will gripe about their 'hood, even whilst strolling through McCarren or dragging their fixie about the sidewalks. The only solution, they decide, to their housing dilemma is to move to the fucking mountains. Build a cabin with no 'lectricity and rough it—even though the most experience these kids have had with camping was that trip to the park grounds last weekend when everyone tripped on acid and Dan and Ratter got naked and ran into the road, and Betsy got so drunk they had to take her to the ER. Ah, nature.

"While visiting home is mostly a dark and depressing experience, one trip to the thrift shop at St. Jude's really lifts my spirits. I fucking love this place. There's the faint smell of vintage, the clueless old volunteer clerks in sweatpants clucking around and slapping $4 price tags on Ferragamo ankle boots, the grocery baskets from the '80s piled by the door, 8-tracks, cracked china and, in the very back, the fucking Elysium of consignment clothing.

You wouldn't believe the shit I've got from here, and people constantly comment on it, and I'm all, 'Oh, small-town Virginia' and they look disappointed and attempt to find the same style at UrbO for about 900 percent what I paid. Standing here with my empty basket and no one around but middle-aged moms in snow boots, I seriously come close to feeling a stirring of the ventricles. Ah, Jesus. I'm almost *happy*.

Wait. Who the fuck is that? Who the fuck is that over there by the window? In the sparkly sweater? And the—Christ, those are skinny jeans. OhfuckhellpleaseJesusGodno. Definitely a 20-something with admittedly OK taste pulling out a—noooo, is that a sea foam green vest with beading at the collar? Put it back! How did you hear about this place! Why are you touching my (future) shit! What the fuck—fucking poseur with your tacky, tacky, while-at-the-same-time-super-expensive Native American–inspired earrings—don't you know this shit is for *poor* people? Like me. Dude, I had to give up lattes for a week to afford this middling shopping spree, and now I'm cranky, super hungo and you're touching my vest. Jesus, this is like a fucking social injustice."

—Deliah L., 29, Apple Genius and barista

WHEN SHIT BECOMES TOO MUCH OF A SCENE

Oh... well. I just thought it would be easier than taking the bus, but I can see what you mean. Do you go to a lot of shows around here? Where's good to go?
I used to go to shows more, but then it seemed like people were going to concerts to be cool, not because they liked the band. It's too much of a fucking scene.

Oh. OK. I get that. I feel like that at shows sometimes. But, you know, I like seeing bands live sometimes... so what do you do for fun?
I mostly just spend a lot of time by myself...
Ah.
...but that whole loner thing is starting to become too much of a scene.

CVS (ALSO, DUANE READE AND, TO A LESSER EXTENT, WALGREEN'S)

Have you ever seen a true hipster in a chain pharmacy? Clutching a red basket and waiting to check out amongst the razors, batteries and faint smell of deodorant? No, because they'd rather support the local economy and stop at the bodega by their apartment to buy condoms, ice cream sandwiches, Orbit gum and a 40 of Sparks (ironically, of course) from their good friend Ramon. He jokes about their creative hairstyle and puts napkins in the generic "Thank you!"–emblazoned plastic bag, and that's something Donna at CVS would never do. Plus, Ramon's Hand-E-Mart makes the perfect spot to get smashed between boozy gallery openings and 9 p.m. open bars on Thursday nights.

CHAPTER 6

AMENITIES

[CASE STUDY]

Every time Leroy C. has a new visitor inside his apartment, he's immediately asked, "Did you just move in?" Leroy's answer: "Nah, man. I've lived here for... seven years now?" Leroy's abode lacks many typical accouterments, but does contain a whole mess of booby traps, such that navigating your way through his living space is akin to going after the Lost Ark (see: *Indiana Jones*). Let us tour via annotated blueprints his actual apartment:

Pools of water in the middle of the bathroom floor. "Yeah, some pipe somewhere is leaking. I'll call the super tomorrow. Just avoid that spot right there, where there's a tile missing."

A veritable shitstorm of nonfunctional lamps and light bulbs. "I'm sorry. I'm too fucking short to reach the overhead light. Here. Take this flashlight."

Lack of proper privacy. "I know, it's totally weird that I don't have a door. I put up a curtain last week, but I stepped on it when I was drunk and that was the end of that. I told my roomie you were coming over, so we should be cool for 20 minutes or so. Let's just make this quick."

Inaccurate timepieces. "I can't figure out how to reset that shit. Just remember that it's an hour ahead and subtract accordingly."

Malfunctioning electronics. "Sorry, the Internet isn't working anymore. That dude we were stealing it from moved. We can go to the coffee shop downstairs and yoink their wireless, but I don't have any money so you'll have to get me a latte."

While we've already broken down the neighborhood and basic dwelling situation of your common hipster (see Chapter 5), we have yet to delve deeper into the bowels of his native environment. Most of humankind functions by way of the nesting principle, seeking to add more and more possessions to one's dwelling space as a way of making it habitable, welcoming and an appropriate locale for cocktail functions, dinner parties and watching *Lost*. Surplus funds go toward the latest and greatest electronics, the most expansive sofa and scores of knick-knacks, such as Precious Moments porcelain figurines.

In this way, one establishes a sense of permanence, home. Like weary pilgrims stepping onto a foreign shore and claiming it by way of planting crops (putting down roots, if you will), most work toward achieving a living situation in which all needs are met in a suite of rooms: nourishment, entertainment, sexual pleasure and the fabled home office. Heck, most of the country would happily move into a self-sustaining biodome if that were a feasible option.

The hipster, however, would rather exude an air of being in transit—you know, like a hobo. To a hipster, settling down indicates that you have reached a metaphorical end stage; you have fluffed your tail feathers and lowered yourself onto your glistening nest egg, content to warm your bones by the hearth of matching china and purring housecats until Death comes creeping to your bedroom door. But as we know, a hipster is always seeking something larger, shinier and more magnificent. He is driven more by his inner whims and desires than by his need for things (with the exception of narcotics, cool new headphones and Salvation Army clothing).

Therefore, a home becomes merely a place to rest one's head. One does not have time to watch the latest hot block of primetime programming when one is always hustling toward artistic genius. (Besides, one can always catch up on *America's Next Top Model* via Megavideo.com at 4 a.m.—for free, at that.) Although a hipster's home is often slowly going to seed (light bulbs guttering into darkness, dirt caking the floors, cheese moldering in the vegetable crisper), the hipster does not care. In his mind, those four walls only amount to a pit stop, so even if he occupies an abode for years, he will never acquire proper kitchen utensils (he cannot cook, anyway), receptacles for his clothing (the floor works just as well) or any of the other niceties of home, aside from the occasional housekitten.

Moreover, there is an underlying laziness[19] that prevents a hipster from acquiring a dining room table or a new shower curtain. This ennui often wears the mask of martyrdom. As we've discussed, a hipster's daily calendar is as changeable as the colors of a particularly pollution-spun sunset. Although he may swear he will make the trek to Target tomorrow to purchase an air conditioner, he will likely either fail to muster the strength to board the bus, or he will be distracted by a party or a vigorous bout of collaging. Consequently, he will put off the task until "tomorrow."

In the meantime, he will begin to adapt to the intense summer heat; what's more, he will begin to *look down* on those who complain about the intense summer heat. He will come to enjoy the feeling of suffering, and of disdain for anyone who wastes the copious electricity necessitated by central air. The lack of this amenity becomes a badge of honor, and the hipster decides he does not, in fact, need such a frivolous nicety.[20] Besides, by the time he works up the energy to actually make it to Target, winter has come and his apartment is shrouded in a cold chill. At this point, he begins the process anew with such amenities as space heaters, extra blankets and warm food.

---

19 In addition to restlessness, poverty and a total inability to plan.

20 Consider it the polar opposite of compulsive hoarding, conceptualized as "a multifaceted problem stemming from: (1) information processing deficits; (2) problems in forming emotional attachments; (3) behavioral avoidance; and (4) erroneous beliefs about the nature of possessions" in a paper published in the journal *Behavior Research and Therapy*. Interestingly, though hipsters suck at acquiring shit, many of the same characteristics seem to apply.

MICROWAVES

Extreme hipsters consider microwaves just another obesity-causing invention that modern society has convinced us we can't live without, like washing machines, Big Business, automobiles and health care. (*Pay $900 a year when I can theoretically visit the free clinics [or just have Mom pay for my dentist visit when I go home]? Fuck that.*) Hipsters show off that additional counter space with pride. (It's there somewhere, I swear, under the two-and-a-half-foot-tall Tower of Pisa of crusted-over dishes.)

"Wow. What a fine selection of movie posters you have. Am I correct in noting that they all feature the films of Robert De Niro? Well, isn't that lovely? You truly have created a singularly glorious color scheme that in no way resembles the dull greens, blacks and reds found in most popular video games that prominently feature handguns and hookers. Cozy. And, no, your ardent love for *The Matrix* is neither trite nor exhaustively obvious. Perhaps we could even watch it later on that mammoth flatscreen TV, hulking there in the corner next to that rather sizable video game console. I could relax luxuriously on this leather couch (still reeking of the poor animal that was forced to give up its life so that you could put the moves on Trixies who get all embarrassed when the leather squelches with their every motion), put my feet up on this futuristic-looking glass coffee table laden with vintage *Playboys* and partake in a Coors from that sweet mini-fridge.

And, if you're really lucky, maybe we will take this party over to your king-sized bed, which appears to be laden with more pillows and cushions than my Aunt Margie's nursing home twin. I severely doubt that you hand-crocheted those black leather numbers, though. Am I right? I assume that you will have to remove each and every pillow first, though, thereby creating enough room to—Oh, wait…what the fuck am I saying? There's no way in hell that I would ever sleep with you. I will take that Coors, though."

—Tulia L., 28, bike messenger and dancer

TRADITIONAL CLOTHING RECEPTACLES

Clothes on the floor   A hardwood floor conveniently serves as both hamper and dresser to a hipster. Outfit-making is easy when all your options are equally crumpled, easily spotted and all sporting an identical film of cigarette ash and dust.

Clothes on the bed   These were peeled off and intended for the laundry after the owner thoroughly dampened them at Pete's dance party (where the impromptu jazz saxophone/acoustic guitar battle was so vigorous the group sweated out all the whiskey they'd consumed). But now that he's grown accustomed to the smell, he's loath to remove the heap, which doubles as an extra layer on chilly nights.

Clothes on the windowsill   The owner's not sure how these articles ended up here (maybe during that drunken hook-up with Jess?), but they've been serving as a nice window insulator for several weeks now.

STUFF HIPSTERS HATE

IKEA

Hipsters truly have a love/hate relationship with that Swedish pleasure palace known as IKEA. While they delight in the low, low prices ($14 for a coffee table! Crazy!), delicious meatballs and cornucopia of weird food with Swedish labels, the store itself is basically one big hipster panic attack waiting to happen. What with the lack of natural light, towering ceilings and confusing products (*Where the fuck are the curtains?! What is this metal thing over here next to this pile of other metal things?! Do I really need this sponge?!*), in no time at all, the average hipster goes from skipping down the aisles, bursting with feverish delight, to rocking back and forth in the "As Is" section as Smash Mouth's "I Can't Get Enough of You Baby" issues from the overhead speakers.

"No, I do not own a television. I feel like American society is far too focused on the specter of the TV set—it looms in the center of the living room like some great all-consuming beast that the entire family is forced to bow down and pray to each night for at least three hours. Moreover, the majority of the programming is either unoriginal or just plain fucking annoying. Maybe if the slobbering masses tore their eyes away from motherfucking hospital dramas every once in a while and read a book, our country wouldn't be so woefully ignorant. Besides, I can watch anything I want on Surf the Channel, and I only ever really watch *Gossip Girl*, anyway...and *90210*...and some stuff on ABC Family 'cause it's so fucking weird...and the *Wonder Years*, now that all six seasons are up on YouTube."

—Jordie H., 28, silk-screener

FLUORESCENT LIGHTS

KASEY: Why is it so dark in here?

MARJORIE: Oh, the overhead light burned out, like, three months ago. I have this really awesome table lamp I found on the street, though, see?

KASEY: Why don't you change the bulb? I mean, how can you see anything?

MARJORIE: I dunno. Haven't got around to it. Anyway, I hate that fluorescent shit—it reminds me of, like, institutions and hospitals and stuff.

KASEY: You mean well-lit places?

MARJORIE: Yeah, but places like that are so sterile. God, why must we have the lights on all the time, anyway? You know, like in grocery stores where they leave the lights on all night? That's so fucking wasteful. In the old days, before electricity, farmers went to bed when the sun went down because it was dark and that meant the day was *over*. Why the fuck can't we do that?

KASEY: Wait, you want to be a farmer?

MARJORIE: It was a metaphor, Kasey. Whatever. I mean if I had my way, life would totally be *Barry Lyndon*, 24/7.

KASEY: *Barry Lyndon*? What the fuck are you talking about?

MARJORIE: Kubrick. Watch a fucking movie. [The room goes dark.] Fuck! The fucking bulb burned out. Fuck this—let's go to Sawyer's place. He has Rock Band.

Let's go for a walk through your unfriendly neighborhood hipster's digs. You'll notice a heap of unwashed dishes creeping about the kitchen, a bathroom coated in hair, grime and curls of soap, and, underfoot, a veritable casserole of clean clothes, dirty clothes, scraps of scrawled tablature, condom wrappers and art supplies. The hardwood floor is a minefield of empty beer bottles, the inside of the fridge hosts several undiscovered species and the only things not covered in a quarter-inch of dust are the reading chair, the stereo and the MacBook Air. Why the voluntary squalor? Simple: Hipsters hate getting artificial chemicals anywhere near their precious immune systems. (Weed, tobacco and shrooms are fine because they're *natural*.) Windex, Simple Green, even that weird canned air—all laboratory made, based on difficult-to-understand voodoo hard science, and all probably responsible for the ADD, asthma and attitude problems of today's addled youth. True, hipsters could buy the eco-conscious green stuff, but Method's gleaming bottles flout two principles at hipsterdom's core: 1) Never buy into whatever marketers are telling you, and 2) Don't spend money on shit, ever. Unless it predicates the quality of an epic, epic bender.

" 'Duuuuude, you gotta check out my ridonkadonk living room set-up, it will fucking change your life, bro. Check it: ultra-high-resolution picture from a Sony SRX-R110 Digital Cinema Projector. Stewart 18-by-10-foot Snowmatte 1.0 Gain fuckin' laboratory-grade screen. Audio fuckin' perfectly balanced with solid-state and vacuum-tube amps, and yep, that there is a Sony BDP-S1 state-of-the-mother-fuckin'-art Blu-ray player. Notice: PlayStation 3, Toshiba HD-XA1 HD DVD player, fuckin' Mark Levinson N° 51 DVD/CD Media Player, Pioneer HLD-X0 Hi-Vision HDTV MUSE

Laserdisc Player, sick Theta Digital Generation VIII 32-bit 8x Oversampling Dual Processors and a fucking 8.8 channel audio system with fucking sixteen 18-inch subwoofers. This thing is *beast*. I hit play and chicks just *rip off their clothes*, bro.'

Ugh, the sad reality for my broham cousin is that this stupid-ass waste of approximately a year's public school tuition will just provide a new location for him to watch *Boondock Saints* with his fellow ogre friends and like, whack off to porn in high-def. Sigh. Whoa, where the fuck is my dog-eared *Roads to Freedom* set? Who the fuck took the Sartre off my bookshelf? Liza's coming over later and I need my existential literature in place and highly visible if I'm gonna get laid, yo."

—Sebastian R., 28, museum docent

BRENDA: I am so fucking hungry. Let's stop at the taco truck at the Woods.

ANN: Didn't you eat dinner? I made myself this kick-ass feast from the farmer's market over in McCarren.

BRENDA: Well, I tried to make dinner tonight, because, like, it felt like springtime outside and I was feeling all productive and get-back-to-nature-y and shit. At first, I totally wanted an artichoke. Like fucking craved an artichoke. So I go to five different little grocery places looking for one, but I think they're out of season? So then I decide I totally want some Bi Bim Bop, and I'm standing in the store trying to remember what goes in it. So I just grab all these vegetables. But when I get home, I look up a recipe, right? On the

Internet? And, like, I don't have soy sauce… or eggs… or any meat… or any, like, knives to cut up all the shit with, so I've just got this huge pile of veggies and, like, a bottle of vinegar.

ANN: Why didn't you go back to the store? I mean, you can buy all that shit at the store.

BRENDA: I used up all my fucking food stamps!

ANN: So you didn't eat anything?

BRENDA: I had a few bowls of Froot Loops…

ANN: Dude, you're gonna get scurvy.

BRENDA: No I fucking won't. They're Froot Loops, man, the name alone implies that they are an excellent source of vitamin C.

ANN: Oh come on, asshole. The taco's on me. Lack of nutrients has obviously addled your brain.

BRENDA: Awesome, but… instead of a taco, could you make it a whiskey shot and a PBR? Thanks.

REAL BEDS

Everyone wants a pillow-top king, right? Wrong. Although the majority of hipsters probably grew up lolling around on a canopy bed in a sea of stuffed bears and turtles (desperately asking God why, at 16 years old, they still have not had their first kiss), when they strike out on their own the lack of a "real" bed becomes a rite of passage. Be it someone else's couch, an air mattress or a frame-free twin haunted by spirits from the great beyond, a fucked-up bed is far preferable to anything Sleepy's can offer. *Bonus:* If you have a shitty enough sleeping arrangement (i.e., your "wall" is a sheet and your "room" can only be accessed by a ladder) your current lover will either A) beat a hasty retreat and thereby avoid the dreaded awkward brunch, or B) invite you back to her place and feed you. Score.

CHAPTER 7

MONEY AND WORK

[CASE STUDY]

Milo K. grew up in a small town just outside of Chicago, Illinois, and from ages six to ten he harbored a serious desire to become a Boxcar Child, i.e., to rough it with his brothers and sisters, cooking potatoes over an open fire and then seasoning them with salt and butter. By age 12, Milo realized that this was not a feasible desire (not for lack of abandoned boxcars, but for lack of siblings), and decided that he wanted to be a bassist in a rock band, much like his idol du jour, John Taylor of Duran Duran. Milo's parents, an environmental lawyer and a cardiologist, told him to "follow his dreams" (since they could not, having been reared by first-generation Russian-Americans who fought in WWII, subsisted on cabbage and never properly learned to speak English). Consequently, they provided him with the requisite lessons, garage in which to practice and '76 Gibson Grabber.

> "Following his dreams" resulted in Milo dropping out of art school at the halfway point because the student body comprised "a bunch of fucking preening bullshitters who don't get music." He moved to a loft in Bushwick where his room consists of a broken, sagging futon, got a job at a brunch spot on the Upper East Side where he begrudgingly serves mimosas to ladies in Chanel, and now saves up his tips to pay for studio space. His band is currently unsigned, but his boss at the restaurant keeps telling him he's got serious potential to someday manage the joint. Milo currently subsists on Cup Noodles and feeds his growing alcoholism by befriending bartenders. He shuns "nine-to-fivers" and summarily dismisses any friends who return to school in order to gain the training required to have a "real career." "Fuck careers," he says. "I'm way fucking smarter than any of those assholes. I've read *Ulysses*."

When encountering Brooklyn's service industry, it is important to note that none of those hardworking hipsters are actually baristas, bartenders or waitresses. No. They are artists. Serving you whiskey/lattes/eggs is just a boring task they deign to perform until their music/painting/writing career takes off. They will follow their paint-splattered dreams by any means necessary, even if that means holding down a job that requires no education whatsoever.

While the denizens of Wall Street and the like aspire to a secure future complete with a loving spouse, romping children and HDTVs with 3D functionality adorning their walls (testaments to their burgeoning wealth), a hipster merely aspires to be "fulfilled." And if that means working at a hipster-douche bar filled with cracked-out NYU students until 6 a.m. every night, then so be it.

Indeed, hipsters are not content to "live and let live"—to accept that we are all on different paths and that some paths culminate in a 401K. Instead, they openly disdain anyone who reeks of being "financially secure" or of "wearing suits." While hipsters secretly envy those with a steady paycheck ("Hey, I guess if I had the choice, I'd rather not hide from my rent-grubbing landlord while walking my lady out in the a.m. after spending the evening blasting Motown and watching YouTube videos"), they would sooner sell their tortured souls than join those rank ranks. In fact, if you were to tell a hipster that you work at a hedge fund or are on the fast track at a women's fitness mag, his response would most likely be: "Pfft. Drag, dude." [See Figure 8.]

But reigning supreme over the urge to avoid sell-out-dom is the need to live a romantic, storied existence—an existence that provides ample anecdotes with which to impress other hipsters and with which to feather their artistic nests.[21] (NB: A good portion of hipsters are not, in fact, destitute. They are often assisted by their parents, who unwittingly send weekly checks that keep their children stocked with beer and narcotics. Still, these hipsters often feign poverty, all the while downloading huge numbers of jams from iTunes and buying countless shirts at Beacon's Closet.)

---

21 Recent research in the *Personality and Social Psychology Bulletin* indicates that workers who are paid an hourly wage (rather than a salary) feel their earnings have a stronger impact on their mental state, likely because they truly grasp each hour's worth. When your hourly wage is barely minimum, it breeds the necessary angst to fuel the great American novel you're writing while off the clock.

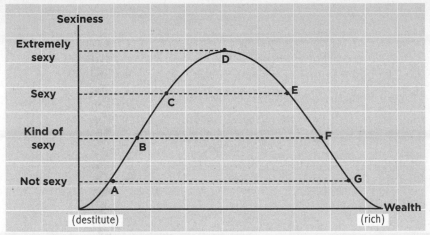

Figure 8: Poverty as It Relates to Sexiness

A. Not Sexy: Dude is 26 years old and still lives at home. He is basically a nonentity.

B. Kind of Sexy: Dude is currently living on unemployment, sleeping on an air mattress in his semiplatonic best female friend's bedroom. He keeps all of his clothing in a suitcase under said girl's bed and spends his days perched in a tree in McCarren Park, taking photos of the nannies that assemble there daily. He lives on Apple Jacks and gets sick frequently.

C. Sexy: Dude is a barista at your local coffee joint by day. By night, he attends college, where he is going for his Ph.D. in postmodern American literature. He lives in a loft in Bushwick in a "room" that he built out of plywood, and wears the same filthy plaid shirt on an almost daily basis. He subsists on hot and sour soup and whatever beer his pitying friends are willing to supply him with.

D. Extremely Sexy: Dude tends bar by night while laboring over massive installation pieces constructed out of animal fur and glass shards by day. He lives in an 8x10 room in which all he has is a mattress and a bookshelf. His limited wardrobe is hung up on the walls like art, and he only has enough coin for one real meal a day (and a steady supply of PBR).

E. Sexy: Dude works full-time as a freelance graphic designer. He lives in a loft with three roommates and has a rather sizable wardrobe that consists of carefully chosen accessories (hats, waistcoats, various and sundry scarves). He subsists solely on takeout and whiskey.

F. Kind of Sexy: Dude owns his own video production company that he launched at age 26. He lives by himself in a one-bedroom, fully decorated apartment, complete with an entertainment system and cat. He regularly cooks for himself and strives to eat only organic and local foods. Wine is his beverage of choice.

G. Not Sexy: Dude works as a day trader in Midtown. He lives in a new high-rise glass condo all by his lonesome and orders all of his clothing from stores like Neiman Marcus. He has his jackets tailored and always appears immaculately groomed. His food arrives via Peapod, and he regularly stocks his fridge with ice-cold bottled beer, which he swills while watching football on his wall-sized flatscreen.

How did that state of affairs come to be? We define the urge to live below one's means as "The Bukowski Syndrome."[22] Charles Bukowski is a veritable hipster hero: a man who struggled under the yoke of laborious oppression, only to emerge years later with a brilliant body of anguished work (ever read *Post Office*? It's a hard road, friends). To stray from these artistic, freewheeling ideals, to loosen oneself from the bounds of the service industry and cast off one's artistic dreams in favor of a desk job and health benefits is to completely forsake oneself, to give up, to sell out. And there's nothing a hipster hates more than a sell-out.

---

22 Bukowski syndrome: Symptoms include restlessness, trouble sleeping, persistent alcoholism, a tendency to wander aimlessly from job to job, a predilection for nebulous romantic relationships and a severe to dire smoker's cough.

"What do I do? Well, Tuesdays and Thursdays I bartend over at a place on Bedford, Mondays and Wednesdays I work as a real estate broker, Fridays I design websites with my freelance graphic design company, and, when I have time, I pursue my true passion: recording my first album with my indie electronic screamo band, We're All Going To Die Someday. I also write epic poetry and make collages for a 'zine that we hand out in McCarren during adult kickball games."

—Anthony C., 25, unemployed

"Jesus, Lord, God, Almighty (whom I totally don't fucking believe in), don't let me see my balance. I'm just gonna blindly punch in my code and wait for the sweet whooshing of those two twenties coming down the chute. Fuck, fuck, fuck—just tell me when it's over. I'm gonna push some buttons. Is the screen clear? Am I good? Fuck, I'm hyperventilating. All clear? Sweet. Let's get wasted."

—Alonna Z., 20, communications student

"Fuck, every time I talk to my mom on the phone she devotes, like, nine minutes to updating me on who's going to medical school where and how their year's going and shit. I'm sorry, Mom—I know you didn't picture me barbacking and working for that sketchy moving company at age 27. But med school? Christ.

Beyond my general disdain for health care professionals (who just, like, poke you and charge you a lot of money and tell you to stop drinking so much and shit), med students are annoying as fuck. They're the high-functioning duders and sorostitutes from college on the one sure path to a fucking three-car garage, under the good-guy guise of wanting to *help humanity*. ('For a while I thought it was my calling to go into Christian education, but then I realized I could witness in a way that's better suited to my gifts by becoming a highly paid surgeon,' blah blah blaahhh.)

Med students also:

* Wear stupid scrubs in public—without irony

* Get wasted on the weekends and post 800 drunk pictures on Facebook every Monday

* Drop medical references and/or anatomical jokes they know you will not understand into totally incongruous conversations, just so they can patronizingly explain them afterward. (Seriously, I don't care what a renal pelvis is or why that's a play on words. Fuck you.)

* Constantly complain about their huge mound of homework

* Try to hit on you at the pharmacy while in their head they're clearly thinking, 'Can I mention med school? What about now? What about

150

now? OK she sort of mentioned Tylenol...can I casually drop it? Damn I am awesome.'

Even worse: students of podiatry, orthodontics and dentistry. Don't even pretend there's motivation there other than cash. Just admit you're a greedy ass-clown and be done with it."

—Christopher E., 27, barback, laborer and painter

WHERE A HIPSTER'S MOST RECENT PAYCHECK IS STOWED

One twenty in a battered copy of Jack Kerouac's *Maggie Cassidy* in the living room, under the couch.

Seven crumpled ones on the dance floor where said hipster tore it up to '60s go-go jams last night.

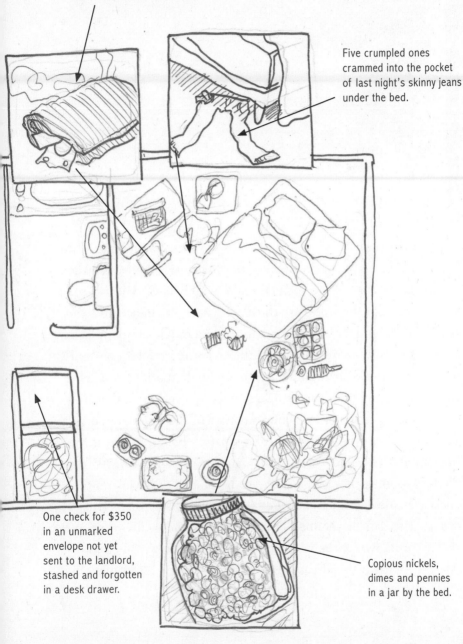

Two twenties in a battered wallet, sandwiched between a couple of old condoms on the floor next to the bed.

Five crumpled ones crammed into the pocket of last night's skinny jeans under the bed.

One check for $350 in an unmarked envelope not yet sent to the landlord, stashed and forgotten in a desk drawer.

Copious nickels, dimes and pennies in a jar by the bed.

AUTHORITY

While hipsters would have you believe that their hatred of authority stems from some deeply noble place—a wholesale rejection of the Darwinian principle of the survival of the fittest, a holy campaign against the elitists of the societal realm who believe that those who succeed in the world are those who have the means to—the reasoning behind this disdain comes from a much simpler place. Hipsters want to feel special, and they want to be told (constantly) just what marvelously unique and exceedingly sparkly snowflakes they are. When one is toiling away under an overlord known as a boss, catering to his or her whims instead of the more mercurial ones woven into the very fabric of a hipster's being ("What if I want to paint all the walls, like, fucking magenta? Really, *ochre*? Who the fuck wants *ochre walls*?"), one runs the risk of having one's cuddly, creative spirit demolished by the glistening Mack Truck that is authority. This is yet another reason you'll find so many hipsters unemployed, where the only authority one has to pay heed to is oneself—and he/she already thinks you're fucking awesome.

JANELLE: Hey dude, Jason is having a fucking awesome party tonight at some loft in Bushwick. Wanna get there early? Like 1 a.m. or somethin'?

TYRON: Sorry, lady. I have to study.

JANELLE: What the fuck do you have to study for? You've been outta school for five years....

TYRON: The LSATs.

JANELLE. Are you shitting me?

TYRON: Naw, I mean, this whole poet thing isn't really working out. I mean, no one wants to pay me to write, so I figured I would, like, learn a trade.

JANELLE: Are you going to be an LSAT tutor...?

TYRON: No, asshole. I'm going to law school.

JANELLE: What the fuck? When have you ever expressed interest in the law? You don't even like motherfucking *Law & Order*—and there are, like, six versions of that show to choose from.

TYRON: Well, lawyers make a lot of money, which is something I don't have. I can't shelve books forever, Jan. I can't. I need stuff like, I dunno, a room with walls. Last week I brought this chick home and she took one look at my so-called room—a shower curtain and bed sheets—and announced that she had to get up early. She's an art handler. How many art handlers do you know who have to "get up early"? I can't deal with this anymore, dude. I need to eat. I need to get laid. I need cash. I mean, yeah, I would probably have to wear a suit year round to cover up my sleeve tats, and, sure, I would have to shave more often and probably move to Manhattan and drink with I-bankers at shitty places like Tonic, and I would most definitely have to pretend to get excited about sports and shit—but I can do it. I can suck it up. I'm almost 30. It's time to get serious.

JANELLE: Dude, you're not going to get into law school. I mean, that's just a stone cold fucking science fact.

TYRON: Why the fuck not? I got like fucking straight A's in college.

JANELLE: Well, for one, you majored in abstract sculpture and Victorian poetry, and two, the most experience you've had with the legal system was that time you got arrested for breaking into that construction site, getting smashed and passing out in your own vomit.

TYRON: Dude. That was, like, a fucking minor offense. Like, you know, a misnomer.

JANELLE: Um. I rest my case.

WORKING AT CHAIN STORES

While myriad hipsters work in retail and/or the service industry, you'll find nary an h-girl or h-boy working at a chain store (e.g., Target, Key Foods, Starbucks). You see, to a hipster, a position folding clothes or frothing cappuccinos at an indie business is merely a romantic interlude on the way to musical stardom/a Pulitzer/a tragically hip death in a Williamsburg loft. Such offbeat occupations have a certain ephemeral appeal: One quickly becomes a tragic everyman, much too sultry and quirky to labor behind a counter for the rest of one's days. In such a role, one may beguile customers and coworkers alike, making the gig a catchall for a hipster's three primary urges: acquiring food and drink, generating angst and getting laid.

Conversely, working at a chain smacks of permanence: the daily ritual of donning uniform and nametag, the coffee breaks with Joan (she's worked here for 15 years—she's a lifer), the total and complete inability to blast one's jams/show off one's tats/get stoned in the bathroom during one's lunch break. (And, lest we forget, the complete and utter lack of attractive people.) The admission that one works at Target is like a pair of carpenter khakis—you ain't gonna find a hipster who'll want to get into those pants.

Notable, yet nebulous exceptions: Scenesters often work at stores like Urban Outfitters or American Apparel—you know, stores that hold open auditions for employees. Hardcore hipsters, however, consider such vocations to be, well, douchey.

Hipsters do not enjoy wasting money on frivolous things such as sustenance. When caught at the crossroads between the taco place (i.e., the place where dinner can be procured) and the bodega (i.e., the place where 40s and Parliaments come from), the bodega will almost inevitably triumph. After spending several long hours listening to records that seem to narrate one's life, the urge to drink one's face off and forget that the world exists usually wins out over any lingering hunger pangs. Besides, there's always a generous supply of dumpster bagels available for the taking—provided they're rat poison–free.

"I picture a day at the stock market going down like one big fucking basketball game—but everyone's, like, really out of shape. There're all these dudes yelling and grunting and leaping in the air, their greed-tinged voices echoing into the abyss, mingling with the squeak of their wingtips as they stomp and pirouette across the floor. Everyone has this vaguely evil odor—like sweat (which has already soaked through their yellowing undershirts) mixed with expensive bourbon mixed with pure, unadulterated money-lust. And it, like, permeates the mahogany-paneled chambers like the rank reek of mildew that works its way into Carson's cabin up in the Hamptons during the off-season.

Everyone's got their eyes fixated on this board, and the glowing numbers that flicker across it like so many wasted dreams totally and completely dictate their happiness, their passions, their fucking *loins*, man. Those dudes totally get off on it, you know. The mob mentality. The futile efforts to spear the golden ring like a child circling round and round on this motherfucking carousel called life. To win, man. If I ever succumb to anything reminiscent of that zombified state, that pure, frothing hunger to reach some horrifically bloated ideal, please put a bullet through my already-departed brain.

The only thing even remotely redeemable about the whole sordid game are those fucking sweet jackets that day traders wear—you know, like with those mesh panels and kick-ass neon tones. Imagine how fucking awesome it would be to kick down Bedford in one of those bad boys. Seriously, dude, that would be a whole new level of badassery. Jonas thinks he's such a free fucking spirit for sporting that Revolutionary War—esque overcoat he yoinked from that thrift shop in Philly. A fucking day trader's jacket would be just the ticket to wipe the smirk off of that unoriginal asshole's mustachioed face. Match and point, man. Match and point."

—Gabe H., 31, cashier at a boutique and percussionist

BUSINESS CARDS

First off, in order to have a business card, one must have a business, and, as we have previous established (see page 147), hipsters rarely do. Business cards, for the rest of society, are a method by which to make connections, to tell the world who you are, what your deal is and, most importantly, how to contact you for future business-related interactions. Let us suppose, for a wild, sweet moment, that a hipster were to take the time to have such a card printed. That he took the trouble to select the font, watermark and ever-important paper weight. Well, we imagine said card to look a little something like the below:

A. Although the hipster's name is really Phineas Martin, this is the name that currently adorns his Facebook profile and, he thinks, best encapsulates his puckish nature. If this moniker proves too much of a mouthful for you, you may henceforth refer to him as M&M—because he "melts in your mouth and not in your hands." Yes, that is a sexual innuendo.

B. Translation: He's currently collecting unemployment, and sometimes his friend who owns a bar down on N. 6th lets him DJ when the regular guy gets too drunk.

C. All attempts to call M&M will prove futile, as he does not enjoy talking on the telephone, which he often forgets to charge, anyway. You're better off e-mailing homeboy, as he is constantly welded to his MacBook Pro. Why the archaic e-mail server? Well, Phineas fails to trust Google's "do no evil" song and dance and suspects that the search giant is plotting to totally Big Brother—out someday and enslave us all using the vast amount of information that it's currently storing up. M&M has several other intriguing theories in this vein, which he will dispense in writing for a small fee (hey, it's business, man!) if you choose to contact him further.

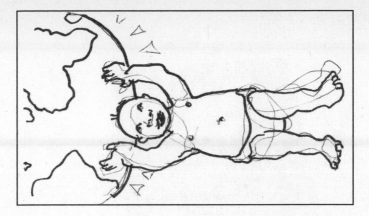

The illustration on the back of the card has no special significance. He drew it on a napkin when he was stoned and was totally stoked on it at the time.

MATH

Numbers + required use of left brain hemisphere + teachers' dirty looks – any room for creative expression = 0 ... interest on a hipster's part in figuring out the bill. He's slapping down a crumpled wad of ones no matter what he owes.

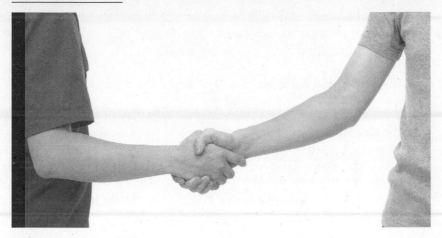

ROGER: Hi, my name's Roger.

MEL: Hey.

ROGER: Um, what's your name?

MEL: Mel.

ROGER: So, what publication do you work for?

MEL: *Occam's Needle.*

ROGER: Ohh, sounds dangerous. What kind of magazine is that?

MEL: It's, like, a poetry magazine for tattoo enthusiasts. Basically, the whole concept is that we should be fighting against the notion that the easiest way is the best way. Like, you should always take the bramble-wreathed path. Always. Writing is pain and so is getting inked. And we should embrace that.

ROGER: Oh… Cool… I work for a magazine called In Tents. It's a camping magazine.

MEL: Ah.

ROGER: But, you know, I've always been really into poetry. I would love to talk to you more about your magazine and what you're looking for in terms of submissions. Do you guys take submissions?

MEL: Yeah.

ROGER: Who would I submit them to? You?

MEL: There's an e-mail address on the website. [Looks over Roger's head toward the exit/open bar.]

ROGER: Ah, sweet. 'Cause, you know, poetry runs in my family. But I've always been too scared to pursue it, because my cousin's in this, like, huge indie band that's all over Pitchfork and whatnot. He's, like, this genius lyricist. I mean, he's playing South by Southwest this year and basically everyone talks about him like he's Yeats or something. So talented. It's cool, though, because he always gets me tickets to his shows and when he's in town we end up hanging with all the bands. So that's pretty awesome.

MEL: Oh… What did you say your name was again?

CHAPTER 8

MUSIC AND ENTERTAINMENT

[CASE STUDY]

Mikey P. is what is commonly known as a "music snob." In fact, if we attempted to explicate here what kind of music Mikey likes, those selections would already be passé by the time this volume hit the peer-review circuit. Suffice it to say: If you've heard of a band, it's highly likely that Mikey doesn't like it. (In that way, this hipster fully lives up to the reputation of the identically monikered boy from the Life cereal commercials).

As a child, Mikey often suffered hard knocks for his unusual tastes. At age six, he developed a strong predilection for David Bowie, a musical selection that garnered the scorn of his classmates, who much preferred the more mainstream stylings of the New Kids on the Block. Still, rather than folding to cultural pressures, Mikey chose to "hang tough." At one juncture, a bully pushed Mikey against a locker and exclaimed,

> "Don't you know David Bowie's gay?" Mikey merely jutted out his chin and responded, "No. He's *bi*."
>
> As a psychologist might predict, once Mikey extricated himself from the bowels of suburban Texas and relocated to the sunnier cultural climes of Greenpoint, Brooklyn, he took on the bullying nature of his former oppressors. Although he relents that his Pitchfork-loving, Pool Party-frequenting compatriots have "alright" musical taste, he cannot stand to let anyone else near his turntable (yes, turntable), and often spends entire parties hunched in the corner, sifting through records in order to select the perfect jam. When "partying" with Mikey, it is important to note: No requests will be taken. In fact, Mikey once ordered a close friend to leave after he asked Mikey to play Jay Z's "Empire State of Mind."

Recall that by very definition, a hipster is a connoisseur of the arts—at least, he likes to think he is. As loath as some people are to admit it, the taste of this sometimes insufferably selective minority strongly impacts what mainstream culture listens to, watches, reads and adopts as culturally relevant. Still, as soon as the average American gets "hip" to a book, movie or band that hipster culture holds dear, said book, movie or band is cast off like the mechanic's jumpsuit introduced in Chapter 3 (see page 60). Why? Because the hipster often operates by the Negative Space principle: One of his favorite ways to set trends is by telling people what *not* to listen to/read/watch.

While the rest of society will turn to such authoritative sources as the *New York Times'* book list, *Rolling Stone* or The Academy for guidance, as soon as a well-known body espouses a creative output, the majority of cool-hunters rush to shun it. The trick is to discover a cultural entity before it makes it big.

Take, for example, a band called "The Skills"[23]—an appropriately nebulous name that could have various interpretations. Let's imagine that The Skills comprises three young men, Trevor, Parker and Billy, who supplement their income by doing freelance web design, copy-editing and bartending, respectively. On the weekends, they play friends' loft parties, functions that they lure their associates to with the promise of coke.

Now let us suppose that a small group of kids sees them play at one of these parties, locates their MySpace page and listens to their jams on repeat. These fans continue to go to their shows as The Skills book bigger and bigger venues—Pete's Candy Store, Cake Shop, Brooklyn Bowl, Bowery Ballroom—until their album hits Pitchfork and gets a glowing review. A hot feeling of jealousy invades the diehard listeners' chests when they hear their favorite song[24] at local coffee shops. The trendsetters listen to the disc less and less frequently, and when their friends put it on at parties they can only mutter bitterly, "God, I knew about these guys when the only people in the audience were me and the fucking bartender." After "Darkness Sleeps So Softly on Your Windowsill" finds its way onto a commercial for the next insipid Apple product, our ahead-of-the-curve music snobs thoroughly loathe The Skills, whose members have quit their menial jobs since reaching "the Big Time." [See Figure 9.]

---

23 As stated before, were the authors to name specific cultural references at this juncture, such indie darlings would be laughably "over" by the time this went to print, so allow us to fabricate a band for the sake of explication.

24 "Darkness Sleeps So Softly on Your Windowsill"

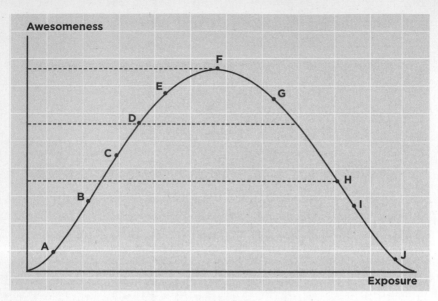

Figure 9: Venues and How They Relate to Coolness

A. Playing accordion on the L platform: Pathetic, but admirable
B. Playing a friend's loft party: No one's listening, but less pathetic
C. Opening for a CMJ band at an illegal music venue: Respectable
D. Playing at an illegal music venue: Cool (bonus points if the cops break it up)
E. Playing a show at one of Brooklyn's more popular venues: Cool, unless it costs more than $5
F. Actually playing at CMJ or Pitchfork: Pretty fucking cool
G. Playing Bonaroo: We're glad you're touring, but, seriously, fucking *Bonaroo*?
H. Playing a show in Manhattan: Seriously, you expect me to cross the bridge to see you play the same three fucking songs you played at CMJ? And at Brooklyn Bowl? And in that totally emo video on Pitchfork?
I. Playing from the speakers at a local bar: Don't you go to this bar? Isn't this embarrassing for you? Oh wait, you're on fucking tour. Too good for BK, huh?
J. Playing from the speakers at American Eagle: I don't go to American Eagle, but if I did, I would be fucking livid.

Hipsters are exclusive, jealous beasts. You may think they would wish only success on bands (and authors and indie film producers) they admire and adore—after all, in many cases the artists clinging to these dreams are their close friends or, oftentimes, themselves. But in reality hipsters will summarily dismiss someone or something they once held dear when said thing "sells out." Why? Again, hipsters are "interested in new and unconventional patterns." Once a band[25] has been adopted by mainstream society, it is no longer "unconventional" nor "new." It is accepted, integrated into the world that the hipster is striving to escape by scrabbling toward the horizon of artistic expression.

This process is actually necessary for society to create novel and varied forms of entertainment. If there weren't some subset of the population as continuously disappointed, eternally fickle and intrinsically ADD-afflicted as the residents of the hipster realm, the entertainment sphere would constantly be replete with moldering cultural geriatrics pumping out one tired product after the next.[26] The sad byproduct, however, is that the hipster exists as a perpetual malcontent, and hanging out with such a terminally unimpressed specimen is like passing an evening with Hamlet: lots of whining and more than a few suicide attempts.

---

25 Note that hipster elitism shines most clearly in their musical selections. While plenty of hipsters are literature or film snobs, those predilections are more nebulous—some hepcats love adrenaline-soaked blockbusters as much as art house cinema, and while some h-kids only read books you've never heard of, others gleefully embrace Harry Potter. But they're all music snobs. Every. Last. One.

26 Somehow Bob Dylan has managed to hold on, but there are exceptions to every rule.

Yeah, hipsters may Torrent with the best of them, but they *hate* purchasing digital music. If they had their druthers, we would never have moved beyond vinyl—something they will tell you repeatedly as they flip through their stack of worn records, searching for the perfect LP with which to seduce you whilst drinking sickly sweet wine from teacups. Still, in true hypocritical hipster fashion, homeboy totally has an iPod (complete with big-ass, brightly colored headphones), which is basically welded to his head at all times. How else can he compose the soundtrack of his life—listlessly riding home from Red Hook, The National wailing into his embittered ears about how Ada has left it all up in the air? But everyone knows that such exquisite pain sounds much better when scratched out of a 10-inch sheet of plastic.

J. D. Salinger's *The Catcher in the Rye* is one of the most mystifying additions to the hipster's canon of hatred. After all, Holden Caulfield is the *original* hipster—one might even expect him to be their poster boy. Perhaps the similarities are too much to handle. Perhaps their hatred springs from the fact that we were all forced to read said book in high school, and any mention of high school unearths a plethora of scarring memories. Or perhaps it's just because Holden ends up in an asylum in the end ("Hey, we're *eccentric*, not batshit *insane…*"). Either way, this is a curious state of affairs considering how many traits Holden and hipsters share. Observe:

1. He is a talented and intelligent artistic soul who hasn't lived up to his full potential and doesn't know exactly what to do with his life. That's the textbook definition of a hipster. I bet Holden grew up to be a freelance programmer and guerilla installation artist (after he flew the cuckoo's nest, that is).

2. He generally pans anyone who shows an interest in athletics (I don't buy that he

left those fencing foils on the subway "by accident"...). Hipsters don't really engage in any sports except those that children enjoy, and they shun any form of musculature (see page 94).

3. He doesn't feel any compulsion to ascribe to conventional fashion mores—witness the red hunting cap, which he wears in his own very special way. We've already seen hipsters sporting said hat when the weather turns chill, and sometimes even on decidedly mild days when an outfit needs that extra punch.

4. He hates "phonies." See: Everyone who doesn't live in one's hipster ghetto and many people who do.

5. He frequently romanticizes the opposite sex, fixating on one small charming aspect of a woman's manner (She keeps all her kings in the back!), but never musters up the courage to go after that particular girl. Instead, he calls up the broad who says "grand" (which drives him insane) and ends up in a dramatic, meltdown fight with her. Which is why the entire hipster race will either die out or settle for a "phony" and move to Park Slope.

MISSED CONNECTION: I was reading a dog-eared copy of Middlemarch, you were clutching a lump of cold, unyielding metal…– w4m – 29 (L train)

Date: 2010-06-17, 3:15AM EDT

Reply To This Post

I'm sorry… are you reading a book or surfing the web or playing fucking FarmVille or some such shit? How the hell am I supposed to know? I mean, I thought you were kinda cute when you got on at the Halsey stop with your uke strapped to your back. I find tiny instruments so fucking hot. But… then you took out that particular tiny instrument (no man, get your mind outta the fucking gutter). Jesus! How much does that fucking thing cost? Like five hundred fucking dollars? That's, like, two months rent, man! God, I don't spend more than $10 on anything. (Except my iPhone. And my MacBook Pro. But that's it. Also, this kick-ass pair of vintage boots. Oh, and these headphones. But sound quality is fucking important.) I mean, dude, I could tell you that I was the chick reading a dog-eared copy of Middlemarch, but how the fuck am I supposed to describe you? The homeboy who appears to have a musical soul, but for whom words are merely pixels and electronic ink? No, bro, I don't think I want to find you after all. I'm just gonna surf my way over to the m4w section and see if that dude who was reading The Sorrows of Young Werther outside of El Beit has posted anything for me, the chick who still digs going to the library. Dude was rocking a motherfucking typewriter, man.

• it's NOT ok to contact this poster with services or other commercial interests

PostingID: 1633299829

Irrespective of how good it is. Hipsters have been listening to these guys for years, and they like their old stuff better. Observe:

Basement recordings [critical reception: nonexistent]   Though no one will uncover these tracks until the band is hard at work on its third album, hipsters will talk about their possession of these recordings constantly and with a heavy dose of smarm while vaguely promising to burn a copy for you. After extensive surveys, the authors have yet to find a single instance of this promise's fulfillment.

First album [critical reception: minimal]   With its quiet release and "raw," unproduced sound, this album is every hipster's favorite. Though his CD player is covered in dust, a hipster keeps the jewel case from this purchase on his rack to prove via price sticker that he bought it at Atomic Records in the mid-'90s.

Sophomore album [critical reception: positive]   This album spews from the band's flashy new label just as mainstream America perks up its ears to the sounds of the earlier CD. Reviewers call it "mature, polished." Hipsters call it "a fucking shame."

Third album [critical reception: disappointed]   This album follows an eight-year hiatus that included the band's sequestering and a public split from their label. The hiatus killed it for everyone: critics are disappointed and hipsters have long since moved on. When pathetic hipster lites discover the band for the first time and eagerly ask their more legit friends if they've heard of them, they are subject to an intense beam of Hipster Hate in the form of a Look.

Fourth album—independently released LP [critical reception: positive]   Critics say they've "returned to their roots." Oddly, at this point the music snobs begin lauding the merits of the "underappreciated" second album.

Anything released postmortem   Gospel. Pure gospel.

"Oh, Christ, is that girl over there having a seizure? Someone should, like, grab her and hold down her tongue with, like, a swizzle stick or something. Wait…Oh, fuck—is she *dancing*? Really? Like, right up in the guitarist's face? What the hell? Is she *waving her hands in the air* like she just don't fucking *care*? Is this, like, a fifth grade dance at Cedar Lakes Junior High where someone spiked the punch and little straight-edged Sarah got unintentionally smashed and tried to grind with the foreign exchange student, Gunther, who ran to the bathroom and cried because his body is changing? No…I'm pretty sure that this is a Yo La Tengo concert, and I'm pretty sure that Ira would rather not see that chick's uvula bouncing up and down as she belts out 'Autumn Sweater' and gyrates. No, dude, *uvula*—like, that thing in the back of your throat. Although I'm sure he can see that, too—she just attempted to do the twist. Ah, fuck, dude—why do people like that have to kill my buzz by coming to shows? I'm just gonna stand here in the front row and keep my face totally expressionless—that way those lyrical geniuses up there will know that I'm *serious* about my music."

—Stanley F., 31, short-order cook and cartoonist

"All I want to do is buy one of the CDs currently lined up in front of Jeffrey Lewis, who is totally bad-ass enough to sell his own merch. The line isn't that long (due to the woeful ignorance of the majority of the American public when it comes to good music—they're probably all drooling over motherfucking Coldplay at some shitty arena). I'm almost there. The awesomely

D.I.Y. disc is within my grasp—and then, *he* steps in front of me.

'Hey, Jeff!' he says in an overly familiar voice—a tone that suggests that this hunched figure in scuffed green Converse has been friends with the indie musician since they were in preschool, that they used to build peanut-butter-and-Saltine-cracker towers together at the Lewis family kitchen table while giggling over Mrs. Lewis's Victoria's Secret catalog.

'Jeff, awesome show, man. I loved that song about mosquitoes. I had a mother of a skeeter bite on my ankle last week and the swelling still hasn't gone down. Hey, hey, hey, Jeff, I gotta ask you. I have to know. Did that girl from the "Chelsea Hotel Oral Sex Song" ever, like, contact you? Because I totally had a similar experience where I wrote this ironic poem in Missed Connections to this chick who works at Greenpoint Cafe and—'

Anger sears up through the soles of my Vans, worming its way in a hot channel through the legs of my skinny jeans until it comes to sit,

Alien-like, in my stomach. I fight the urge to smash this dude in the head with my carabiner. I imagine him dying in myriad horrific ways— one of which involves a freak lightning strike that connects with that silly earring hooked on his lobe (does he think it's, like, 2003?).

Finally, homeboy attempts a complicated handshake with the confused musician and shuffles away, probably with a tent in his Levi's, fucking kiss-ass. Here's my chance—I see the CD resting gloriously on the merch table. I raise my eyes to meet Lewis's, open my mouth to speak, tell myself I'll keep the interaction to a contained and slightly aloof token of praise. The CD is in my hand. Lewis is looking at me. The dude behind me coughs a slightly annoyed cough. 'Hey, Jeff!' I say."
—Crispin C., 26, music writer and bicycle repairman

SONGS THAT INSTRUCT YOU TO MAKE SPECIFIC MOTIONS

Including (but not limited to):

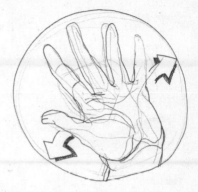

*Clap your hands

*Wave your hands in the air

*Shake it/work it/twirl it

*Get low

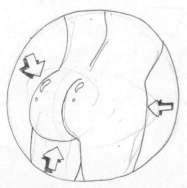

*Anything to do to or with your ass

Notably exempt: '80s rap

ARTEMIS: Jesus, I was at this terrible fucking club last night—they charged ten bucks to get in because there was a "DJ," but all he did was play shit like "Sunday Bloody Sunday" at a volume only feral dogs and babies can hear.

ZEPPO: Heh, feral babies… I just picture them foaming at the mouth. Oh, dude. I had to go to a U2 concert once.

ARTEMIS: You *had* to? Did someone threaten to cut off your balls with garden shears or something?

ZEPPO: No. It was my little sister's birthday. I had to, like, chaperone. I dunno what the fuck is wrong with that little brat—she just, like, lies under the kitchen table singing "Hold Me, Thrill Me, Kiss Me, Kill Me" for hours at a time. I think my mom dropped her on her head when she was baby.

ARTEMIS: She does have a weird-shaped head.

ZEPPO: Yeah. It was awful. It was at, like, Madison Square Garden and everyone was, like, crying and smiling and singing along. And they were *clapping*. You know, like, clapping along with the beat. Like they all felt like if they somehow didn't participate in the horror that was going on stage, they would cease to exist. I hate when people clap along to the music. It's not like it's a Raffi concert. They're just gonna, like, fuck up the jam. I mean, if it were possible to render a U2 song any more fucked-up than the original. Anyway, at one point, one of my sister's little friends just, like, takes a break from roaring the words to "With or Without You" and turns to me and goes, "You look really unhappy." And I was. I was so. Fucking. Un. Happy.

ARTEMIS: I feel you dude. I hate U2, too. Anyone who likes U2 should be sterilized.

ZEPPO: Um… my sister likes U2.

ARTEMIS: Yeah, but…

ZEPPO: Should my sister be sterilized?

ARTEMIS: No….

ZEPPO: Well, man, I mean, it's fine for people to like U2. It gets some people off, right? It totally gets my sister off. She fucking loves that shit—consumes it like food. I mean, I hate U2, but I feel like if it makes people happy, then fine. I mean, I hate when people judge people for liking shit. That's just seriously fucked-up.

"The absolute worst fucking part of braving Goodwill for some sweet new blazers and grandpa sweaters: the incessant, cranked-up KissFM DJs, tumbling out of the store speakers, yammering on in their suffocating idiocy. Never mind their nasal tones and their struggle to read the morning news and traffic reports without stumbling over the big words. Forget their complete lack of a college education and their threadbare grasp of politics, 20th century history, even basic geography. ('Archipelago? I think that's a type of dictatorship.') No, the truly insufferable aspect of every blubbering, moronic, overly enthusiastic ass-clown with a headset and microphone is that *arrogance*, that total delight in running contests and getting calls from preteen fans, that sugary glee that comes from listening to themselves speak. Really, the only thing worse than morning show DJs are the stupid motherfuckers who call in. Christ, those people who dial in should be fucking flagged for immediate departure to Gitmo. Polluting the radio airwaves is a crime against fucking humanity. If only every DJ were as awesome as my buds Kasia and Liam. Their show, 'Pretentious Indie Suckfest,' streamed online at 3 a.m. Thursdays and sometimes illegally downloaded from the web and transmitted over the air as an unlicensed service (the FCC fucking *hates* that) is the only thing outside my iPod I can stand."

—Bianca Z., 21, Victorian literature student

"Unfuckingbelievable. I bring over farm-fresh Strawberry Cough and you repay me by making me sit through *Old School*? Are we pubescent boys coming to term with strange sensations in our groins? Are we lounging in Tarrah's basement and her mom just brought us pizza bites and we're all arranging ourselves in a coed puppy pile in order to feel like we're sooo tight while secretly hoping to cop a scary and confusing feel? No? Then why the fuck are we sitting here stoned out of our minds, two steps away from dead (no, literally, sleep is the only state in-between, I'm talking fucking *science*) and consuming this pathetic tribute to guzzling beer and seeing boobs? This is completely illustrative of a repressed nation's attempts to fucking reclaim their wasted adolescence by focusing on tits like sterile bottle-fed Neanderthals. It's sick, man. It's fucking sick.

What do you mean? What the hell does it matter that all my freelance fashion photography is of topless women? That's fucking *art*, man. Now hand me another beer."

—James G., 28, silent film pianist, photographer and book assistant

ROLLING STONE: *"RS* is for aging dad-jammers who dig yacht rock but still feel the urge to cling to their last vestiges of youth. They know everything about the latest tween queen on the virginal sacrifice block, but nada about actual music. Jesus—it's like the print version of MTV, but with more dry, political stories accompanied by nauseating cartoonish graphics. I'd rather spend all day at a mall record store, listening to slow-jamz on those nasty headphones—same experience, but I'd save five fucking bucks and maybe grab a pretzel."

PASTE: "Hmm, used to be cool… the downloadable tracks sound kinda sweet, but they're hiking the price up substantially. I'll just write down the track list and Torrent it when I get home."

RANDOM INDIE MUSIC MAG: "Oh man, I would totally buy that, but that asshole Marcus writes for them and if I wanted to read his preening bullshit, I would just surf on over to his pathetic Tumblr and pore over his dreadful personal narratives. I really enjoyed that one about how he hooked up with that merch girl while she was touring with whatever the fuck that SXSW band was and then decided his life was empty and that he should just quit his fucking job and go live for a year in some rural town with a waterwheel. Well, guess what? He's still fucking here. And he still has that fucking job. Meanwhile, he keeps saying *my* pitches need more focus. I'll show him focus—I'll focus my weed onto his fucking story and my lighter to the edge of that fucking page and just focus on the wall for a while."

"Ten years from now, this convoluted, overexposed excuse for entertainment could very well be the next *Twin Peaks*. But now it's just another thing that bros and Trixies can celebrate each week with a fridge full of Amstel Lights, Domino's pizza laden with meat products and a typo-riddled Facebook invite titled something along the lines of: 'Season Final: OMGGGGGGG I dunno how I'm gunna survive until next season without this genus show!!!' Yeah, sorry, not even gonna dignify that one with a negative RSVP—just gonna let it hang in the social networking ether like one big 'I don't care.'

I mean, really, what is this? Some kind of cult? Will there be ritual sacrifices of young goats while some bro pretends to be what's-his-face and some girl pretends to be what's-her-face and then they, like, act out the sex scenes that they wish had happened last season? Honestly, I don't begin to understand your rabid obsession with this insipid, idiotic piece of truly ephemeral, plasticine pop culture. Naw, man, I'm just gonna hit up two-fer Tuesday, stumble home drunk and watch reality TV— that shit's actually got some oddly deep social commentary, if you really think about it."

—Gigi Q., 25, decoupager and community organizer

CHAPTER 9

PHILOSOPHY AND BELIEFS

[CASE STUDY]

According to Jackson M., there is no God. It's as simple as that. And he will frequently announce this fact to devout friends and relations in order to make them uncomfortable/spark debate/assuage a bout of intense boredom. He didn't always feel this way: jaded, cold, entirely impassive to the religious themes in the films of Ingmar Bergman. Although he was raised a good Catholic boy in the mountains of Sequim, Washington, as soon as he traded in kneeling before crosses for kneeling before the communal acid cup, he concluded that there was less in heaven and earth than is dreamed of in our feeble philosophy—which he majored in during college.

The fateful moment of nonbelief came one night in the woods, when he and his friends were seated around a crackling campfire, contemplating doing a rain dance to rectify a particularly intense drought

> that was seriously hampering their efforts to grow pot on the soccer field. A doe wandered into the clearing, blood gushing from a hole in its side—obviously the byproduct of a hunter's shoddy aim. The deer fell to the ground near the fire and uttered its last dying cry. The assemblage decided to toast its demise with a shower of PBR from their nearly empty cans. As Jackson watched the stream of cheap beer soaking the deer's dappled coat, cascading into its glassy eyes, he decided that no God in heaven could have created such a sad, cruel excuse for existence. Jackson often tells this story to girls in order to sleep with them.

Nonreligion is merely one realm of the hazy collection of convictions and beliefs that make up the average hipster's theology. Karl Marx once said that religion is the opiate of the masses, which indicates that your average prole is perfectly content to exist on a steady diet of, essentially, one big downer. The hipster, by nature, is not OK with being perpetually sedated (at least for long periods of time).[27] Hipsters seek to live in a dangerous and changing world, replete with twists and turns and fantasy and excitement—a fictionalized existence that shifts and churns like the liquid globules inside a lava lamp.

Hipsters thus reject the serenity of conventional religion, choosing instead to live by a seemingly arbitrary collection of beliefs and convictions.[28] But peeling back the plaid veil, one

---

27 Despite what The Ramones may say.

28 Research from the journal *Mental Health, Religion and Culture* indicates that both religious folks and those who simply believe in a "higher power" are more likely than

realizes hipster dogma centers on antithesis. One does *not* believe
in God, one does *not* accept traditional gender roles and one does
not strive for wholesome and fulfilling romantic relationships, all
constructs embraced by our oh-so-structured society. If something
is written down in the Bible, in the history books, or in the volumes
of Miss Emily Post, you best believe that your average hipster will
completely and totally reject it.

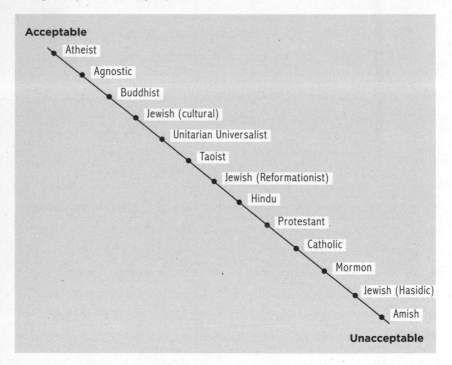

Figure 10: The Acceptability of Major World Religions

As a result, hipsters are, in a sense, the eternal children of our
wasted generation: uncontrollable free spirits dancing toward ruin.
A 34-year-old man may persist in acting like a 17-year-old, downing
shots of vodka at the very unHappy Hour of 8 a.m., chasing dreams
of rock stardom and shunning his parents' suggestions that he find
a "nice girl to settle down with." Such ideas are completely outside

196

his realm of experience, even though many men his age already have mortgages and golden retrievers named Hank and Betsy and kids named Chance and Lassie.

In fact, in the same way there are "dog years," there are "hipster years," which convert in the opposite direction.[29] By blatantly flouting society's rules (which are rife with pesky attributes such as results and effects and consequences), hipsters exist in a state of suspended adolescence. Such a realm is very much akin to Pleasure Island, the mythical, debauched arena that Pinocchio finds himself trapped within after indulging just a little too much. This state keeps a hipster well-preserved until he finally reaches a breaking point (perhaps around age 40). At this point he relents, grows up and rolls the stroller over to Carroll Gardens, his eyes low and his jowls sagging. Either that or he refuses to let go of the shiny baubles of youth and becomes that dude sprawled outside the only cool bar left on Bedford with a sign reading "Sexy and Homeless."

---

atheists to swallow a host of whacko delusions: that computers can control thought, that there are hidden personal messages on television and in movies, and that they are being constantly "persecuted." While every hipster firmly believes the universe swivels around his spindly form, few would wander down that whole "my laptop made me do it" road. (Exception: When they're tripping the light fantastic on some high-grade pot.)

29 For example, a 28-year-old indie dude is really only about 19 in hipster years—still aimlessly staggering about drinking Colt 45 and making poor life decisions.

one of these days i am gonna take that turnpike and just fucking drive

JOB: What the fuck are you doing? Are we gonna stand here and stare at the Five Dollar Footlong ads all night, or are we going in?

LEE: Don't rush me. They have, like, pre-put-together subs, right?

JOB: What? I mean yeah, there's, like, meatball subs. But even if you pick one you have to like, choose the toppings and shit.

LEE: Shit. Is everything listed?

JOB: Like the toppings? Probably. I mean, you can see them. They're right there.

LEE: OK. Fuck. OK.

JOB: Except I guess the sauces. They're sorta unmarked. Dude, the bus stops running at midnight. Fucking go in.

LEE: What sauce do I pick? How do I know which sauce to get?

JOB: Are you fucking kidding me? Just get sweet onion teriyaki. Flip the fuck out. Hurry up, people are starting to stare.

LEE: Sweet onion teriyaki. OK. Sweet…onion…teriyaki.

JOB: Shit man, McGonogle just texted me. We gotta bring beer.

LEE: What brand?

JOB: Your call.

LEE: [passes out]

ENTHUSIASM

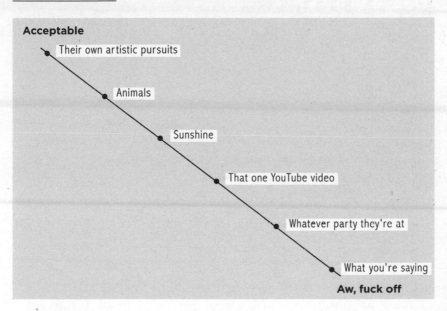

For pretty much, like, anything.

When it comes to their feelings, hipsters are veritable chatterboxes—maybe not always verbally, but bear with us. While most hipsters aren't the type to call up their besties and yammer into the night about their broken dreams, they will engage you in lengthy text convos about their body issues and/or distrust of women; call you when they know you're sleeping to leave you long, drunken voicemails; post yearning Missed Connections to lovers who have spurned them; and habitually write angsty epistles on the bar bathroom wall. If you can't already gauge a hipster's level of sadness by the increasingly pronounced slump of his rounded shoulders, just take a peek in his notebook, which he's likely scribbling in openly while sighing next to you on the J train.

"I'm always fucking bumping into this type—in Salvation Army, browsing through old bomber jackets; in the coffee shop, meandering to find a free outlet; in the used book store, running their fingers over the old yellow paperbacks' spines. They carry around guitars and notebooks and iPhones like normal people. They walk like normal people. But they sure as hell don't talk like anyone I know. They're, like, the fucking 'cool' followers of Christ, and they've basically succeeded in sapping all the fun out of life.

It doesn't take long to out one of these dudes. For a minute, he seems cool. Then you notice his overall enthusiasm, this weird fucking optimism. Your bullshit detector starts letting out its feeble beep, you know? He giggles and tells, like, wholesome stories about that time they all went camping and the girls stole everyone's towels. And then, swear to God, one of two things happens. Either he begins witnessing—a fucking broad swath attempt at evangelism that breeds nothing but awkwardness—or he seduces you with his bizarre cheer and impeccable manners and even agrees to come home with you, suddenly sitting upright on the couch mid-make-out to whisper, 'There's something I have to tell you... I'm a virgin.'

I don't fucking get it. How can one call oneself a functioning human being if one does not get drunk once in a while? Or smoke pot on hot summer nights? Or say 'fuck' when the mood fucking takes you? And in the name of all things holy, how are these people surviving without *sex?!* The junk-showcasing skinny jeans, the sculpted hair, the sullen glances at attractive specimens from the other side of the bus—all for naught. Why they even get out of bed in the morning is beyond me, because there sure as hell ain't anyone warm and mussed and smelling of tobacco on the other side of it."

—Trina B., 24, projectionist and atheist

JOSIE: Hey Ethan!

ETHAN: [heavy sigh] Hey, Josie.

JOSIE: Why the long face?

ETHAN: What are you talking about?

JOSIE: Your face. Just now, you look mad or sad or something.

ETHAN: I was just thinking.

JOSIE: About something sad?

ETHAN: What, is this an interrogation? Do I need to relate a sordid tale now? Christ, are you expecting something about how I didn't get a puppy when I turned eight, and instead I got a fucking trumpet, and I was so mad I threw it on the carpet and I thought it would be fine because it's carpet but the bell crumpled and everyone yelled at me so I'm all fucked up now?

JOSIE: *Sorry*. Jesus. Just wondered if something's wrong.

ETHAN: Do you really want to have a conversation about this? Do you really fucking want to get into all the reasons we should be fucking terrified? Glenn Beck is on TV telling his three million bobble-headed viewers the Three-Fifths Compromise was a step toward abolition, voters are shooting down gay marriage left and right, the ice caps are melting, we're spending more money in the Middle East in a day than I'll see in my entire wasted existence and Sarah Palin's book was a bestseller on Amazon before it fucking came out. We're on the brink of a fucking apocalypse. Anyone who's happy is either deluded, misinformed or just fucking stupid.

JOSIE: …so nothing's up with you today?

ETHAN: Me? I'm actually having a really good morning.

THE INDI-BRO

Main Entry: **indi-bro**
Pronunciation: \\'in·dē-brō\
Function: *noun*
Date: 2009
: an attractive male person who enjoys independent music
and/or culture, but still persists in being a bro. A hipster male
may befriend an indi-bro, but mostly because said bro/hipster
hybrid can get free tickets to shows and/or knows where all
the parties serving free liquor are located. Often mocked
behind his back for his use of hair gel/rippling pecs/secret
love for power ballads, the indi-bro, in turn, uses the hipster
to up his "authenticity" factor.

NOTABLE INDI-BROS

Gabe Saporta: Possibly ironic pop/punk star who enjoys wearing
plaid and silly sunglasses; also enjoys exclamation marks and is
widely known for being a "babe."

Joseph Gordon-Levitt: Reclusive film star who started out "cool,"
appearing in such sleeper hits as *Brick* and *Mysterious Skin*, and
then lost a measure of cred for his role in the aggressively hipster-
marketed *500 Days of Summer*. After appearing on the cover of
Nylon Men, JGL officially sealed his indi-bro status, but managed
to retain some respect for looking like a pale-faced Midwestern
bartender who just took a dip in a swimming pool full of whiskey
and poor life choices.

Chuck Palahniuk: Formerly subversive author with a penchant for
penning cringe-worthy stories involving everything from lullabies
that kill to pool drains that suck out one's insides. Loved by hipsters
for, like, two seconds before publications like *Men's Fitness* called
him out for being quirky and that "first rule of Fight Club" joke was
pulverized like the proverbial dead horse. Plus, check out those guns.

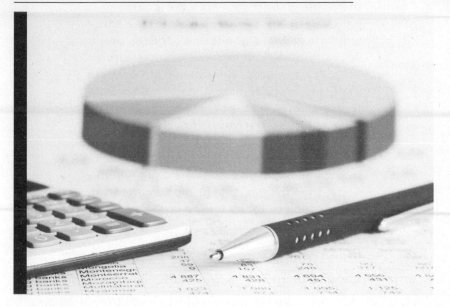

Every once in a while, a brand will attempt to shill its wares to the hipster set, employing pictures of frolicking actors in bohemian clothing, indie background music and/or bold messages about "being yourself" and "wandering off the beaten path." Such advertising campaigns inevitably crash and burn—much like Jonas's old Mustang did when he tried to drive across the desert last summer on a gas tank full of vodka. Why?

1. Hipsters don't have functioning TVs, so it's highly likely that no one in the target demographic will ever see the new alt-music-soaked commercials.

2. Hipsters don't purchase mainstream brands, which are often the culprits in these situations. The bodega down the street doesn't carry Charmin or Miracle Whip; it's all about Panda Soft and Nayonaise, brother.

3. Hipsters refuse to accept that they fit the demographic to which the company is pandering. No, the average hipster often gravitates toward goods and services better suited to other cultures and countercultures. Take, for example, the seemingly endless varieties of caffeinated malt liquors that hipsters often embrace, mostly because of their ability to get you seriously fucked up for very little capital. Though these beverages were clearly created for hip-hop fanboys or something of the like, hipsters chug 'em like nectar from the Gods. Why? Did I mention that they get you seriously fucked up?

In short, if the folks over at, say, Miracle Whip really want to draw the younger crowd into their world of mayo-y goodness, they should hawk their merch at ghetto-ass bodegas slathered on premade sandwiches that are soaked in booze and marketed toward rappers. Mmm, an excellent source of irony.

USING CAPS

While hipsters are usually *huge* sticklers for grammar (never mind their love of ludicrous abbreviations and neologisms), when it comes to using the shift key, it's laissez faire all the way, baby. Ever get an e-mail from a hipster? For those who have not had the pleasure, here is a typical excerpt:

> hey dude, not much is going on here. i've been taking the b62 a lot, just for kicks. i like looking out the window and watching the world spin 'round the sidewalks—all the ghost signs on the facades o' the buildings and the halfway people trippin' down the sides of the highways. you just don't get that on the subway, man. everyone's listening to their music and traveling 'round in their own little orbs—like gerbils in those plastic balls. i'd rather be a rat in the race than a gerbil in a ball. no lie.

Although the epistle may be lengthy with text and full of clever turns of phrase and well-wrought imagery, chances are, not one letter is standing tall. Why? First of all, it takes a lot of effort to hold down two keys at once, and secondly, a string of lowercase text is just, well, much more visually pleasing than the jagged peaks and valleys that constitute a conventional sentence. Also, the caps lock key popped off about two months ago, and the hipster in question has been way too fucking lazy to fix it.

OLDSTERS

One of the main tenets of hipsterdom is, intrinsically, youth. Hipsters are colorful new blossoms careening merrily toward a glorious end. In short: *Hipsters are not supposed to grow up*. Which is why aging members of the counterculture are so reviled: They are grim markers of what looms over the horizon, cautionary tales in the flesh. In general, there are two kinds of oldster:

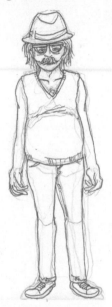

1. The Old Dude at the Bar: A horn-rimmed-glasses-wearing, fedora-sportin', Smashing Pumpkins–adoring loser whose burgeoning gut spills over the top of his skinny jeans like froth over the lip of an overfilled Yuengling. This specimen is most likely an "artist," but, in reality, spends more time drinking whiskey on the sidewalk outside his studio than actually painting. He whiles away his days playing a giant game of musical chairs, moving from neighborhood bench to neighborhood bench, until he takes his rightful place on his favorite bar stool, where he officially kills everyone's buzz.

2. The Hipster with a Baby on His/Her Hip: A wide-eyed host with a tiny person permanently welded, parasite-like, to their body. The hipster parent persists in frequenting the same brunch spots, stores and (rather disturbingly) dives that he or she did before becoming afflicted with infantitis. I'm sorry, Mommy and Daddy, artful stains are cool, but whatever is spewing out of that small keening beast has no place splattered across your totally played-out cowboy boots.

In short, although hipsters live in a state of extended adolescence, if they had their druthers, they would see their elders (read: anyone over 35) meet some dramatic fabled end, or park their skinny asses on an ice float and disappear out to sea...you know, like a dying Eskimo is wont to do.

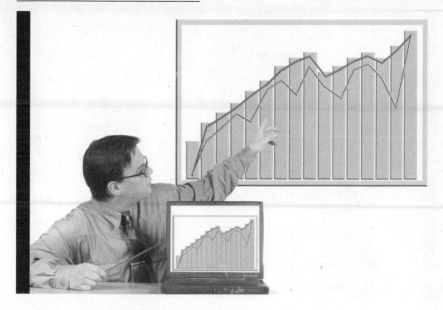

MILLIE: You know that David Lynch–themed bar-slash-gallery idea I was telling you about? I've been talking about it with my friend Clementine and we're going to make it happen, aiming to open the doors by next fall. Her boyfriend's cousin is this crazy-rich venture capitalist and he's totally into the idea, so we're all meeting next weekend to start looking at possible locations. It's gonna be cool. We'll have shows for all our friends, like maybe you and Craig and Woody and whoever else could think about putting something together for the grand opening.

[Six months later]

JONNA: Hey, whatever happened with that bar-gallery thing you were working on?

MILLIE: What the fuck are you talking about?

OTHER HIPSTERS

To be a true hipster, one does not identify oneself as such. That is why you will often hear dudes in skintight jeans and chicks flashing calculator wristwatches muttering, "Fucking hipsters," as they sip at their PBRs and glare at all the NYU kids smoothing their red cigarette pants and spewing off the L train.

How do you know when you've finally arrived as a hipster? When you hate other hipsters.

GLOSSARY

Barnes, Kevin: Frontman of passé but respected indie outfit Of Montreal. Known for sporting multiple outrageous, feathered getups and gobs of glam-rock makeup during the band's incongruently straightforward concerts.

Beacon's Closet: A chain of clothing stores at which you may buy and sell used clothing. Hipsters frequent the stores so often that it's almost as if an entire neighborhood is sharing one, big, slightly smelly communal closet.

Bedford Ave.: Williamsburg's most famous and scenester-clogged artery.

Bed-Stuy: Originally known as Bedford-Stuyvesant, a sketchy Brooklyn neighborhood where only the most hardcore of hipsters hang. It's so in, no one lives there yet.

Bolt Bus: Cheap transportation between the East Coast's major drinking cities. It uses that the-first-few-seats-are-dirt-cheap-so-book-early model. Thanks to their inability to plan ahead, hipsters usually snag the pricier, more last-minute tickets, and thus disdain the line as the more bourgeois alternative to the scary Chinatown Bus.

Bowery Ballroom: Apparently, if you play there you're hot shit. Most hipsters have never been because they hate waiting in line/paying more than $5 for a show/going into Manhattan.

Brooklyn Bowl: Bowling alley/music venue down by the water in Williamsburg. (Generally full of the authors' exes. Generally avoided by the authors.)

Brooklyn Label: Coffee shop frequented by the authors despite the fact that it has the word "Brooklyn" in the name. All employees follow an unofficial rule whereby they must have visible tattoos.

Bros: Light-denim jeans. Polo shirts. Bulging pecs. 401ks. Basically, everything hipsters are not.

Cake Shop, The: Tiny concert venue on the Lower East Side where many famous indie bands once played. They do, indeed, have cake—or cupcakes, rather.

Charleston, The: Otherwise known as "The Gnarlston," a quasi-metal bar on Bedford Avenue in Williamsburg that is frequented by dudes who look like Pete Wentz, and the authors when they are drunk and craving free pizza (which comes with every beer).

Chinatown Bus: Super-sketchy transport from New York City to exotic locales such as Boston and Philly. The bus of choice for cheap hipsters who don't want to shell out the extra four bucks for the Bolt Bus, which has wi-fi and doesn't necessitate a cautionary tetanus shot.

Clem's: A boring Williamsburg bar. Unremarkable except for its hot bartender.

CMJ: Short for "College Music Journal," a weeklong fest held by a publishing/events company in New York every fall. One attends shows (and open bars) via RSVP, so if you spend any money during CMJ, you're doing something wrong.

Crusties: A merry assemblage of punks who hop freight trains in order to attend shows across the country. They often forgo such luxuries as showers and clean clothing, and feast on food from the back alleys of eateries—hence the highly descriptive and apt moniker.

Cup Noodles: Hot, salty goodness in a Styrofoam chalice.

Daddy's: A Williamsburg bar with a decent jukebox that's good any night except Saturday, when it suddenly fills with post-show bands and their obnoxious kiss-ass groupies.

Death Cab For Cutie: Super, super emo band that's kind of not cool to like anymore. Every little hipster's soul cries, however, when "Your Heart Is an Empty Room" comes on—because it's *so true*. Our hearts are empty rooms, my friend, our hearts.are. empty.rooms.

Dolphin Hotel: Setting in the novels of Murakami in which strange and fantastical things occur—hauntings, unexplained periods of darkness and visitations by a man dressed as a sheep. All of these things could become manifest at an average hipster's apartment, most likely in the wake of a party.

Dumpster bagels: Often stores cannot sell all the bagels they bake in a day. Consequently, they deposit said bagels in plastic garbage bags next to trash receptacles. Since these pastries don't actually touch the rest of the trash, they are completely safe to eat—and actually quite tasty with a little schmear.

Ed Hardy: A brand of clothing spawned by a tattoo artist of the same name that frequently features rhinestones, Spandex and airbrushed beasts of many tropical ilks. Generally considered "douchey" by the hipster set (and nearly everyone else).

El Beit: Coffee shop on Bedford Avenue in Williamsburg known for its airy back patio, epic bathroom graffiti and spotty wi-fi. Several chapters of this book were composed there. And several awkward run-ins with the authors' exes occurred there during the same period, providing still more book fodder.

FarmVille: Lame game that one plays on Facebook if one is a friendless teenage boy or an overweight Midwestern housewife.

Fugazi: They're, like, totally D.I.Y. punk (or they were—they've been on hiatus for, like, a decade now). Everyone knows that.

Ghosting: A term coined by the authors of this book. The preferred hipster method of ending a relationship. Instead of starting a formal breakup conversation, hipsters prefer to slowly cut off contact from romantic interests until they are no longer speaking. The process is similar to the slow fade of a spirit dematerializing in a haunted mansion.

Greenpoint Avenue: A main drag in Brooklyn's Greenpoint, a predominantly Polish 'hood where hipsters share the sidewalk with elderly Poles and their walkers.

Harem pants: A fashion trend that, regardless of what the street style blogs say, was never embraced in Brooklyn.

Hesse, Hermann: Pretty much every hipster worth his or her salt has a battered copy of *Siddhartha* somewhere in his or her apartment. And pretty much every hipster worth his or her salt has yet to read it.

It's Always Sunny in Philadelphia: Mumblecore-esque FX series about four self-involved and inappropriate 30-somethings who own a dive bar and are terrible people. Thanks to its brilliant ad-libs and totally un-PC treatment of African-Americans, religious people and the mentally handicapped, *Sunny* is actually acceptable to quote in hipster circles.

Jorts: Shorts made from tight, old, cut-off jeans. See also: jeggings, jeedos.

Levee, The: Bar in Brooklyn that provides free cheese puffs, Blow Pops and board games. That's basically all you need to know.

Matchless: Another Brooklyn tavern, best know for its "Two-Fer Tuesdays" and the bad decisions that ensue.

McGorlick Park: A park in Greenpoint near the BQE subway lines. Less popular than McCarren when it comes to picnicking and having sex under the cover of darkness, but still frequented by locals.

Missed Connections: A section on the website Craigslist in which hipsters may channel their most angsty hopes and dreams, describing in lyrical detail men and women whom they admire from afar. Most denizens of Brooklyn scour them on a daily basis, but few will admit to doing so. The authors, for two, hardly *ever* visit this site.

Moleskine: Overpriced notebooks beloved by Ernest Hemingway and the adherents of hipsterdom.

Murakami, Haruki: Japanese novelist who writes about un-extraordinary men who sleep with beautiful women and have adventures. It's pretty obvious why hipster boys dig these books. See: *Norwegian Wood, The Wind-Up Bird Chronicle* and *Dance Dance Dance*.

My So-Called Life: '90s angst fest starring Claire Danes that we all related to sooooooooo much, especially that episode where Angela thinks that Jordan Catalano wrote a song about her called "Red," but it was really just about his car.

N. 6th: An easily accessible street in Williamsburg proper where many of the biggest hipster-douche bars are located (and a terminally bright American Apparel that was once ransacked by angry locals). The hardcore hipster set scorns anyone who lives in the general vicinity.

New York Muffin: A baffling chain of pastry shops with locations in several Brooklyn neighborhoods. Basically a haven for bros, Trixies and the elderly.

Park Slope: Brooklyn neighborhood full of lovely brownstones and quaint shops. Where hipsters go to die.

Pete's Candy Store: Tiny concert venue in Williamsburg where a lot of famous indie bands once played. Sadly, there is no candy.

Pitchfork: An elitist music website that also hosts a concert fest in Chicago. If you are in a band, "making Pitchfork" is at once a blessing and a curse: For that one, shining moment you will be considered a "hipster darling," until, of course, you rocket to stardom, and consequently, cross into the realm of *over*.

Pool Party: Free summertime concerts that used to take place at McCarren Park Pool (hence the moniker), but now occur on a grassy stretch near the waterfront in Williamsburg. Sometimes they get kick-ass bands to play, but if the act in question necessitates waiting in line, you're better off drinking take-out margaritas from Turkey's Nest Tavern and listening to your ghetto blaster in the park.

Red Hook: A cheap, barely accessible area of Brooklyn where IKEA is located.

Royal Oak: A bar in Williamsburg that's so douchey, it's fun. Basically, everyone there sucks, so one just gets super drunk and dances, free of judgment. Consequently, bad decisions are always made.

Screamo: A genre of music that merges metal and emo. Take a moment to conceptualize what this sounds like. If you are imaging a whining teen whose voice has just broken being pummeled with dodgeballs, you're pretty much on the mark.

South by Southwest (aka SXSW): Music festival in Austin, Texas. Basically equates to hipster Spring Break.

Strawberry Cough: A sweet strain of marijuana ideal for old, pretty pipes.

Tecate: Cheap canned beer that's often available when PBR is not. It comes with a slice of lime, which means it's classy.

Tonic: Bar in Manhattan. Sub-par food, sub-par drinks, sub-par atmosphere. Totally on-par with everything a hipster hates in a drinkery.

Torrent (v): To steal music online, basically.

Trixies: Former sorority girls who boast flat-ironed hair, perfect tans and designer bags containing tiny dogs. Such women often have jobs that require them to have pleasant telephone voices.

Trophy Bar: A watering hole in south Williamsburg that used to be fun, then got lame, but is probably fun again by now.

Union Tool: A tavern in Williamsburg whose official name is "Union Pool," but is often referred to thusly because of the number of tools who frequent it.

White hats: Duders who wear those blindingly white baseball caps with stupid logos (e.g., Hollister Surf Co.) on them and listen to Dave Matthews Band.

Wreck Room: A Bushwick bar that features cheap cream beer and myriad games. Although it is located in Brooklyn, it more resembles a Chicago or Boston drinkery—i.e., there aren't that many attractive people there.

PHOTO CREDITS

ACKNOWLEDGMENTS

The authors wish to thank: Our moms and dads, Julia Bartz and Lara Ehrlich and Doug Riggs, Matchless Two-fer-Tuesdays, Liz Davis, the Internet, our readers, Tumblr, Twitter, Facebook, the L train, the G train, the Brooklyn Label baristas, the Royal Joke, McCarren Park, El Beit, Katherine Groth and her camera, kind line-editors Leah Konen and Merritt Watts, "Book Deal Buddy" Lindsey Kelk, the guys at *Death+Taxes*, the lovely people of *SELF*, *Mashable*, *Heeb* magazine, the Astral, the B62 and whiskey.

ABOUT THE AUTHORS

Brenna Ehrlich is a news editor at Mashable.com. A graduate of the Medill School of Journalism at Northwestern University, Brenna has worked for *Heeb* magazine and has freelanced for *Esquire*, *Mental_Floss*, Radar Online, the *Chicago Reader* and *Death + Taxes* magazine. She's a fan of elevated trains and attending concerts.

Andrea Bartz is a news editor at *Psychology Today*. Before that, she worked in the Happiness Department at *SELF* magazine and has written for *Money*, *Heeb*, CNN.com and an array of alt weeklies. Andi grew up in Milwaukee and studied journalism at Northwestern University before moving to Brooklyn. She enjoys wooded parks and good cheese.